The **ESSENTIALS** of
Business Law I

William D. Keller, Ed.D.
Professor of Accounting
Ferris State University, Big Rapids, Michigan

Research & Education Association
Visit our website at
www.rea.com

Research & Education Association
61 Ethel Road West
Piscataway, New Jersey 08854
E-mail: info@rea.com

THE ESSENTIALS®
OF BUSINESS LAW I

Year 2006 Printing

Printed in the United States of America

Library of Congress Control Number 2001091426

International Standard Book Number 0-87891-690-3

What REA's Essentials®
Will Do for You

This book is part of REA's celebrated *Essentials*® series of review and study guides, relied on by tens of thousands of students over the years for being complete yet concise.

Here you'll find a summary of the very material you're most likely to need for exams, not to mention homework— eliminating the need to read and review many pages of textbook and class notes.

This slim volume condenses the vast amount of detail characteristic of the subject matter and summarizes the **essentials** of the field. The book provides quick access to the important principles, concepts, doctrines, and legal terms in the field.

It will save you hours of study and preparation time.

This *Essentials*® book has been prepared by experts in the field and has been carefully reviewed to ensure its accuracy and maximum usefulness. We believe you'll find it a valuable, handy addition to your library.

Larry B. Kling
Chief Editor

CONTENTS

CHAPTER 1

LAW AND BUSINESS

1.1   WHAT IS LAW?

Law is a form of Social Control.

Law is a Rule of Conduct, prescribed by the State, commanding what is right and prohibiting what is wrong.

Law is a set of rules allowing one to predict how a court would resolve a particular dispute.

1.2   THE TRADITIONAL VIEW OF LAW

This view defines law as a body of rules that courts apply in settling disputes.

1.3   THE SOCIOLOGICAL VIEW OF LAW

Supporters of this view say the purpose of law is to promote justice and stability in a society.

1.4   THE FUNCTIONS OF LAW

The functions of law are to settle criminal matters, to settle civil (non-criminal) disputes (such as labor-management dis-

1

putes), to protect private property, to settle contract disputes, to settle property disputes and disputes regarding sales, commercial paper, and business associations, and to protect the State.

1.5   LEGAL SANCTIONS

Legal sanctions are orders of courts, and they must be enforced. Also, the general public in a nation must have a desire to abide by the law.

1.6   LAW AND MORALS

Law is what the courts or legislatures allow people to do, while morals are principles of correct conduct based on customs and religion.

An example of a law that is also a moral is ***Thou Shalt Not Kill.***

An example of a law that does not have to do with morals is driving to the right side of the road.

An example of morals that are not law is not letting a child play in the street.

1.7   THE LEGAL PROCESS

The Legal Process is fairly complicated with several steps. A Civil Action begins with the issuance of a summons or a citation from the court. This is a direction to the ***defendant*** to appear and answer the claim of the plaintiff.

EXAMPLE

The Defendant owed the Plaintiff $200 and the plaintiff received a promissory note as evidence of the debt. When the Plaintiff did not get his money back, the Plaintiff sued the Defendant on the loan and the note. The Plaintiff's written complaint demands $200.

The facts of the Complaint must be proved, either by documentary evidence or by sworn testimony of witnesses at the trial.

Each complaint must have some legal authority behind it.

EXAMPLE

Brown, the defendant, living in California, was sued by Smith, the plaintiff, in a New York court for $12,000. Unless Brown, the defendant, is personally served with process in New York or has property there, he cannot be brought within the jurisdiction of the New York Courts. In addition to this, the New York Civil Court only has authority to try cases under $10,000.

A person does not have to have a lawyer, but if the person does not have one, that person is at a disadvantage. The procedure of a trial is technical and requires a knowledge of the rules of evidence.

Evidence must be **relevant**; that is, it must bear a relationship to the fact that is to be proved.

The Defendant has only limited time after being served with a summons or complaint to answer the summons. If the Defendant fails to do so, a judgment by default may be entered against this person.

The Defendant should get legal advice immediately after being served with a summons.

Both plaintiff and defendant have the right to a jury trial if either requests it.

Preparation for Trial contains the following:

Bill of Particulars is demanded by the defendant and prepared by the plaintiff's lawyer. It gives more detailed information concerning the plaintiff's claim.

Depositions and Interrogatories are methods by which each side may gain more information from the other prior to trial. These are a series of questions to be answered by the party being examined.

Jury Selection is a process whereby jurors are usually selected by lot from a list of qualified residents of the county in order to get a random sampling of citizens.

Depending on state law, a jury of 12 (or sometimes 6) people is selected. Potential jurors are questioned, first by the plaintiff's attorney, then by the defendant's attorney. A juror who states that he or she cannot be impartial will be excused from serving.

Both sides are permitted a certain number of *Peremptory Challenges* which they may use at will without giving any reason. This is a safeguard to eliminate any prospective juror whose attitude indicates bias.

Civil Trial procedure is as follows:

1. The Plaintiff has the burden of proving the elements of his or her complaint. (In a criminal case, the prosecution must prove its case beyond a reasonable doubt.)

2. The Plaintiff's lawyer makes an opening statement to the jury, explaining what he intends to prove.

3. The Defendant's lawyer then makes his opening statement.

4. The Plaintiff's lawyer presents his proof through witnesses and/or documents. (Exhibits)

5. Witnesses are forced into court with a subpoena which is a paper served on them by a court representative.

6. Witnesses are sworn in, promising to tell the truth.

7. The witness is first questioned by the attorney that brought him or her to the court, then cross-examined by the other attorney.

8. The defendant then makes the closing statement (summation) to the jury, summarizing the case and giving his/her side of it.

9. Finally the plaintiff's lawyer will give his or her summation.

10. The judge then instructs the jury as to the principles of the law in the case.

11. The jury retires to deliberate the case. Usually in criminal trials the decision must be unanimous. This is true in many civil trials also, although some jurisdictions now require only 5/6 of the jurors to agree.

12. The jury decision (verdict) is usually *for the plaintiff* or *for the defendant,* although in some courts the jury also determines the amount of compensation.

13. **Appeal Procedure** is provided for. The losing party may appeal to higher court if some error of law was committed during the trial. A notice of appeal must be filed within a limited time. The appellate court will read over the papers filed and may also ask the lawyers on both sides to appear before it.

14. The appellate court will either affirm the decision of the lower court or reverse it and send the case back for a new trial.

15. The **Judgment** is the court decision. If the plaintiff wins the judgment, it will be entered in papers filed in the County Clerk's office. If payment is not made within a reasonable time, an officer of the court may be directed to seize and hold the debtor's property until payment is made or until the property is sold.

1.8   SCHOOLS OF LEGAL THOUGHT

Schools of Legal Thought are ways various courts and lawyers have agreed and differed on in the past, as well as in the present.

The Natural Law School is composed of legalists who wish an ideal state of being; that is, definite right or wrong.

People do not create natural law, but rather, they discover it through the use of reason, and the knowledge of good and evil.

Ethics is the source of legal authority.

Ancient documents such as the Magna Carta, the Declaration of Independence, the U.S. Constitution, and the United Nations Declaration of Human Rights reflect *Natural Law*.

EXAMPLE

"We hold these truths to be self-evident, that all men are created equal, that they are endowed by their creator with certain inalienable rights..."

The **Historical School** believes that Law is an *Evolutionary Process*. The Historical School proponents concentrate on the *Origin* and *History* of the legal system. These ideas are based on the *Legal Principles which have withstood the passage of time*. These ideas follow past decisions of the courts.

The **Analytical School** uses *Logic* to shape laws. They examine the legal code and use *logic* to extract the principles that underlie it. These analysts formulate *General Principles* which then become *starting points for legal reasoning*. Then *Individual laws* are judged as to whether or not they are in agreement with these *starting points*.

Legal Realists believe that Law is an *instrument of social control* based upon social forces and needs. They think that law changes as times change. Thus, the *same conclusion will not always follow* from the same set of facts. Law is legitimate depending on *how well it serves society*.

1.9 SOURCES AND CLASSIFICATIONS OF LAW

Constitutions are documents that set forth general organization, powers, and limits of the government. Laws passed by Congress outside the powers delegated to Congress in the Constitution will be declared unconstitutional by the Supreme Court.

Courts with Federal jurisdiction are those set up by the U.S. Constitution or by laws passed by Congress. (U.S. Supreme Court, U.S. Court of Appeals, Federal District Courts, Federal Tax Court, Federal Patent Court, etc.)

EXAMPLE (FEDERAL COURT CASE)

A murder committed on an Indian reservation would be tried in a federal court, because Indian reservation land is protected by federal (not state) law. Indian reservations were set up by federal government treaties with various Indian tribes.

All powers not granted to the Federal Government are retained by the States or the People (Tenth Amendment to the U.S. Constitution).

EXAMPLE

The U.S. Constitution gives the federal government the right to regulate *Interstate Commerce* (between the states), but the states retain the power to regulate *Intrastate Commerce* (within the state).

The Constitution sets up the three branches of government: legislative (law-making—Congress), executive (law enforcing—the President, cabinet, and bureaus) and judicial (law deciding—the courts), with a system of checks and balances so that one branch cannot dominate the others.

EXAMPLE

Supreme Court can declare Congress' law unconstitutional.

EXAMPLE

President appoints members of Supreme Court with the consent of the Senate.

Statutory Law includes laws passed by Congress and/or the various state legislatures. It also includes **ordinances** passed by city councils and county boards.

Administrative Agency Regulations are rules set up by various agencies of the government, such as the *National Labor Relations Board*, the *Securities and Exchange Commission*, and the *Federal Trade Commission*.

Business Law is the body of law that pertains to commercial dealings, such as Contracts, Partnerships, Corporations, and agencies.

Uniform Statutes are proposed laws drafted by the American Law Institute and the National Conference of Commissioners on Uniform State Laws. Many of these have been adopted by a number of states. They include: Uniform Commercial Code, Negotiable Instruments Act, Uniform Sales Act, Uniform Warehouse Receipts Act, Uniform Bills of Ladings Act, Uniform Partnership Act, Model Business Corporation Act, Uniform Stock Transfer Act, Uniform Consumer Credit Code, and the Truth in Lending Act.

Uniform Commercial Code was written by the National Conference of Commissioners on Uniform State Laws.

— It has been adopted by all 50 states.

— It mainly concerns *legal contracts* and their *enforcement*.

Substantive Law comprises all laws that define, describe, regulate and create legal rights and obligations.

EXAMPLE

In order for a contract to be valid, there must be **consideration**. This means that contract promises are enforced in the court only where each party receives something of value from the other party.

A person who injures another through negligence must pay damages.

Procedural Law (Also called Adjective Law) is the way courts are set up and run. Procedural Law describes how a lawsuit should begin, what papers to file, to which court a particular lawsuit should go. It also describes which witnesses can be called.

Public Law concerns relations between persons and the government. (Criminal Law and Constitutional Law are parts of Public Law.)

Private Law concerns relations between the various persons and their dealings.

Civil Law (Noncriminal) spells out the duties existing between persons, or between citizens and their governments.

Contract Law is part of Civil Law having to do with the enforcement of contracts.

Tort Law has to do with injuries on the job, also customer injuries while using a product, also damage to reputation. Tort means a *wrong*.

Criminal Law is a wrong committed against the public. The Government seeks to impose a penalty on an allegedly guilty person.

Courts of Law can award only three types of compensation: *land, items of value,* and *money.*

Courts of Equity are for people wanting compensation other than land, items of value, or money. Usually they want *specific performance* – that is, they want people to do exactly what they promised to do in the contract, such as paint a picture. Specific performance is usually available to the Plaintiff only under a suit of *breach of contract*, where the Plaintiff claims that the Defendant has not carried out what he or she agreed to do in the contract.

1.10 DEFINITIONS OF TERMS

Statutes of Limitations are time periods for different types of cases. After the time allowed under a statute of limitations has expired, no legal action can be brought no matter how strong the case was originally. These time periods differ in different states, but are often in the neighborhood of 5 or 6 years.

Injunctions are Court Orders to a specific person directing that the person refrain from doing a specific act until the court can make a decision.

Recision is an action to undo an agreement, to return the parties to their status quo prior to the agreement.

EXAMPLE
The seller misrepresents the quality of the goods so the court orders both parties to rescind or undo the contract.

1.11 LEGAL RESEARCH

Lawyers find and analyze case law by looking up past decisions in law libraries.

Most trial court decisions are not published. They are merely filed in the office of the Clerk of Court for public inspection.

Federal Court and New York Court trial decisions are published.

Decisions of appellate courts are published. (These are called **Unwritten Law**, that is, they are decisions of the court and are not laws passed by Congress or by state legislatures.)

11

Appellate Court decisions are numbered and published by the National Reporter System, also published by the West Publishing Co.

Federal court decisions are found in the *Federal Reporter, Federal Rules Decisions, West's Bankruptcy Reporter, U.S. Supreme Court Reports, Supreme Court Reporter, and Lawyer's Edition.*

1.12 BUSINESS AND ETHICS

Many legal cases have evolved because of questionable ethical practices by businesspeople who might think more of profit than of honest dealing.

EXAMPLE (Ethical Questions in Business)

Insider trading, environmental pollution, conflicts of interest, hazards in the workplace, overbilling on defense contracts, check kiting, and consumer fraud.

EXAMPLE (Specific Ethical Duties)

A corporate lawyer has a duty to keep confidential the proprietary information of his employer.

A real estate agent representing a seller must not purchase the property for his own account without notifying the seller.

An automobile engineer with responsibility for design safety must hold paramount the physical well-being of consumers.

EXAMPLE

A lawyer's conflict between the duty of confidentiality and the duty to uphold the law:

A client announces to his lawyer that he plans to lie on the witness stand. (The lawyer is an agent of the court. Does the lawyer reveal this information to the judge? If he does so, his client may in the future not tell his lawyer all the facts because the lawyer has breached his client's right to confidentiality.)

1.13   SCHOOLS OF ETHICAL THOUGHT

Duty-Based Ethics: (Immanuel Kant) An individual must refrain from any action that would become a problem if everyone would do it. Also, it is immoral to treat other human beings only as a means to an end.

Utilitarian Ethics: Acts should be considered according to their effect on society as a whole. We should do the greatest good to the greatest number of people.

Social Justice: How rights, benefits, and obligations are distributed among the members of society. This is based upon **Social Contract** — an understanding among members of society that things should be done a certain way.

Libertarianism: Individual freedom is based on property rights with a minimal role for government. From each as they choose, to each as they are chosen. The wealthy may keep their money; however, they may give charity to the poor if they wish.

Personal Conscience or Individual Responsibility: A morally responsible business is one in which people with high ethical standards are making the decisions.

Examples of Ethical Questions in Business Today:

— Do I take home office supplies?

— Do I falsely call in sick?

— Do I see a colleague steal and not report it?

13

— Do I make personal phone calls from the office?

— Do I overstate tax deductions on my tax return?

— Do I understate income on my tax return?

— Do I make personal photocopies from the office photo-copy machine?

1.14   PRINCIPLES OF BUSINESS ETHICS

Avoid Conflict of Interest: Conflict of Interest is when a business interest is at odds with a personal interest.

EXAMPLE

A corporation purchasing agent selects one of her close relatives as the company supplier.

Three methods of avoiding conflict of interest:

1. Disclose the problem fully to all interested parties.

2. Have an independent party certify to the fairness of the transaction.

3. Have someone else from the firm make the decision.

Honor Confidentiality – Do not disclose secret financial information of the firm; do not disclose secret recipes and the like.

Exercise Due Care – People with more training and professional positions are expected to perform their tasks at higher levels than those required of lay people.

Act in Good Faith – Honor your promises, avoid deceit, behave reasonably, treat others fairly.

Be faithful to special business responsibilities – (This is especially true of trustees, agents, managers, directors, and corporate officers.) Make good on contracts, promises, and living up to professional codes. Satisfy all the expectations of your position.

Respect the rights of others – Do not put people below you on the business ladder in unethical positions. Limit restrictions on subordinates.

EXAMPLE

Should an employer require his or her employees to submit to tests to see if they have AIDS or if they are taking drugs?

Do not lie or be dishonest in business negotiations. Do not bribe.

Do not put misleading information on résumés.

1.15 SOCIAL RESPONSIBILITY OF BUSINESS

Examples of Social Irresponsibility by Business:

— Chemical plants leak toxic gases.

— Defense contractors produce faulty parts.

— Banks launder drug money.

— Firms produce dangerous products that kill or maim customers.

— Profit-Making is All-Important (Milton Friedman). Milton Friedman, the well-known conservative economist and Nobel laureate has challenged the idea of business social responsibility. He states that social responsibility is a subversive *doctrine*, inconsistent with the basic tenets of capitalistic society. He fears that social responsibility will be forced on firms by government fiat.

Some of Friedman's arguments against social responsibility follow:

— Individuals have responsibilities, but corporations do not.

— Corporate executives are hired to make profits within the law.

— Corporate executives should not make decisions about social responsibilities and social investment (like corporate gifts to charity) because those represent tax decisions and are government functions.

— Corporate executives should use Market Mechanisms, not socialistic Political Mechanisms, to determine the allocation of scarce resources.

The viewpoint that corporations do have social responsibilities states that corporations should not only have profit-making as a goal but should include in their goals the *improvement of society*.

EXAMPLE

A corporation has the moral duty to design gas tanks so they do not set cars on fire.

Corporations should give money to charities within generous income tax limits.

1.16 CODES OF ETHICS FOR CORPORATIONS

The Giving of Business Gifts – Although this is often done in foreign countries, the U.S. viewpoint is that it is a form of bribery.

Reporting Violations – A company's code may state that employees will not be penalized and will not suffer retribution for reporting violations.

Unfair Practices – A company cannot pressure employees to contribute to United Way and other charities.

REVIEW QUESTIONS

1. What is the difference between the Traditional View of Law and the Sociological View of Law?

The Traditional View of Law is that law is an instrument to settle disputes, while the Sociological View of Law is that it is to make the people as a whole live together more peaceably.

2. How does Civil Law differ from Criminal Law?

Civil Law settles disputes between people or corporations, while Criminal Law is the State versus the accused.

3. Are morals the same as laws?

They overlap but are not the same. For instance, lying in court under oath (perjury) is both a crime and an immoral act. Telling a lie outside of court may be immoral, but it is not necessarily a crime.

4. Can a person defend oneself in court, or must the person have a lawyer?

The person can legally defend himself or herself, but the layperson does not know all the court rules so will be at a disadvantage without a lawyer.

5. How do depositions differ from interrogatories?

Depositions are *oral* questions and answers between a lawyer and a witness, taken down by a court reporter, that can be used as evidence in the trial, whereas interrogatories are *written* questions and answers for the same purpose.

6. What is the purpose of depositions and interrogatories?

These are methods by which both sides in a case can get more information from each other prior to the trial and thus hopefully cut down the material that needs to be presented in the trial.

7. How are jurors selected?

By lot from residents of the county.

8. How is it determined whether or not to have a jury trial?

If either party requests a jury trial, that party gets one.

9. What is a peremptory challenge?

It is a lawyer's right to remove a prospective juror from jury duty in a particular case for no given reason.

10. Who makes the opening statement to the jury?

The plaintiff's lawyer.

11. After both lawyers have made their opening statements, which case is presented first?

The plaintiff's case.

12. In what order are witnesses questioned?

They are first questioned by the lawyer who brought them to court, then they are cross-questioned by the attorney on the other side of the case.

13. Which side gives the first summation speech to the jury?

The defendant's lawyer.

14. Is a case appealed to a higher court because of an error of fact or an error of law?

An error of law.

15. Are witnesses present during an appeal hearing?

Only the judges and the lawyers are usually present.

16. How are court judgments carried out?

By the sheriff.

17. What is Natural Law?

A definite state of right or wrong.

18. How is Natural Law discovered?

Through reason and ethics.

19. How does the Historical School of Law differ from the Analytical School of Law?

The Historical School believes that law is based on past court decisions, while the Analytical School extracts logical principles that underlie the law. Then individual laws are judged on the basis of their agreement with these principles.

20. What do Legal Realists believe?

Law will change as times change.

21. How are federal courts set up?

By the U.S. Constitution or by laws of Congress.

22. How are state courts set up?

By state constitutions or by laws of state legislatures.

23. Is murder tried in state or federal courts?

Most murders are tried in state courts, but if the murder is on federal property, it will be tried in a federal court.

24. How do states get control of intrastate commerce?

By the Tenth amendment to the U.S. Constitution.

25. What is the system of checks and balances in the U.S. Constitution?

Each of the three branches of the federal government checks on the others to keep them in line.

26. What are ordinances?

Laws passed by county commissions and city councils.

27. Where do administrative agencies get the authority to issue regulations?

From Congress.

28. What is the main purpose of the Uniform Commercial Code?

To make the enforcement of legal contracts the same in all states.

29. How does Substantive Law differ from Procedural Law?

Substantive Law governs the way people must act toward each other, while Procedural Law governs the way the courts are run.

30. What is Tort Law?

It has to do with INJURIES to self, INJURIES to others, or INJURIES to reputation.

31. How do Courts of Law differ from Courts of Equity?

Courts of Law give as judgments items of value, land, and money. Courts of Equity can force SPECIFIC PERFORMANCE of contracts. Today in the U.S. most courts combine both of these.

32. What are injunctions?

Court orders to stop doing a specific act.

33. What is so-called unwritten law?

History of Court Cases and Judgments.

34. How does so-called written law differ from so-called unwritten law?

Written law is passed by Congress or by the state legislatures. So-called unwritten law—even though actually written —is case law.

35. How does Social Justice differ from Libertarianism?

Social Justice seeks the improvement of society, while Libertarianism favors the individual doing what he or she pleases with as little government as possible.

36. What is conflict of interest in a business setting?

It is when a person uses his or her business position for personal gain.

37. Why do individual businesses need to set up their own code of ethics for employees?

So that employees will have guidelines as to what is expected of them by the business.

CHAPTER 2

COMMON LAW

2.1   DEFINITIONS OF COMMON LAW

The accumulated and organized body of previous court decisions, divided into categories according to subject matter.

Judge-made case law which has its origins in the traditions, customs, and trade practices of the people of Britain and America.

2.2   *STARE DECISIS*

Stare Decisis means that the courts decide their present cases in the same way that similar cases have been decided in the past. (Cases in the future which have similar facts will be decided by applying the rule established in earlier cases.)

Advantages of *Stare Decisis* are:

— Court decisions become more consistent and predictable.

— Persons with similar problems are treated equally.

Common Law based on *Stare Decisis* is the same all over

the country.

Common Law is derived from past court decisions which were derived from customs, practice, and common sense in the British Commonwealth and the United States of America.

2.3 COMMON LAW REMEDIES

Money Damages – If one party won the case, the court could order the other party to pay the first person money.

Writ of Ejectment – A written order from a court ordering a sheriff to remove the party wrongfully in possession of the land.

Writ of Replevin – An order from a court (judge) to a sheriff telling the sheriff to seize the item wrongfully taken or retained and bring it to the court for return to the plaintiff.

2.4 REMEDIES IN COURTS OF EQUITY

Injunction or Restraining Order – Temporary Order by a judge requiring a person to cease performing a certain act until the court can hear both sides and make a judgment.

EXAMPLE
Stop tearing down the house with a bulldozer.

Specific Performance – Abiding by the contract as it is written.

EXAMPLE
In the contract, the defendant promised to paint a picture, so this must be done. Money damages alone will not suffice.

Recision – Contract Cancellation.

EXAMPLE

Dissolve the marriage contract through divorce.

2.5   OTHER LEGAL DEFINITIONS

Plea – A lawyer gives a Statement of Law, then an Allegation of Facts (how the law in this case was violated), and a Request for Remedy.

Writ of Habeas Corpus – An order by the judge to the custodian to **produce the body** (to get a person out of jail, out of a mental institution, or away from the care of a foster parent).

2.6   BENEFITS OF COMMON LAW AND *STARE DECISIS*

Stability and Certainty are assured.

Carefully refined, widely applicable, fundamental principles of appropriate human behavior are promoted.

Periodic Examination in the light of new circumstances – Precedents outmoded by change over time can be scrapped and replaced by more enlightened rules.

— British-based Common Law is still the basis for United States court decisions.

— Common Law can be overruled by modern laws passed by Congress and the various state legislatures.

REVIEW QUESTIONS

1. What is Common Law?

Past court decisions in the United States and the British Commonwealth.

2. The U.S. has been a free nation for over 200 years. Is it still subject to the English Common Law?

Yes, insofar as it has not been overruled by constitutional, congressional or state legislative law, or by United States and state court decisions.

3. What is a Writ of Ejectment?

A court order telling the sheriff to remove a person from land.

4. What is a Writ of Replevin?

A court order telling the sheriff to seize an item from the loser of the case and give it to the winner.

5. What is a plea?

A formal statement of a lawyer to the court, giving the law, the facts, and a request for remedy.

6. What are the benefits of the Common Law System?

It provides a stable method of deciding cases based on similar past decisions of the courts both in the United States of America and in the British Commonwealth.

7. What is a Writ of Habeas Corpus?

It is an order from a judge to have a person removed from jail, or from an asylum, or from the hands of foster parents.

CHAPTER 3

CONSTITUTIONAL LAW

3.1   THE CONSTITUTION

The Constitution is the fundamental law of the United States of America and of the various states.

The Constitution is the Supreme Law of the Land. If Congress passes a law that is contrary to some state law, Congress' law prevails.

Judicial Review means that the Supreme Court can declare a law unconstitutional.

Separation of Powers – There are 3 branches of Government: Legislative, Executive, and Judicial. Each branch can function without interference from the other branches.

The Federal Government has powers listed in the Constitution. The Tenth Amendment gives all other powers to the States or to the People.

3.2   FEDERAL COMMERCE POWER OF THE CONSTITUTION

The Federal Commerce Power of the Constitution allows

Congress to regulate commerce with foreign nations and among the States. This is a broad source of power allowing the Federal Government to regulate the economy.

It stops the States from unduly restricting commerce. We have **free trade** between the states.

EXAMPLE

There are no customs stations at state lines. The U.S. has always been within itself a huge **free trade** area. This promotes business and the entire U.S. economy.

The **Federal Government** has used this power to control business if the activity affects **Interstate Commerce** or is in the flow of commerce.

EXAMPLE

Datzenback (Plaintiff) vs. McClung (Defendant). The McClungs (Defendants) owned a restaurant near an interstate highway. White people could eat there, and there was take-out service for Black people. The McClungs (Defendants) did not want the Civil Rights Act to apply to them. Judgment in favor of the Civil Rights Act. The food used in the restaurant was purchased in Interstate Commerce, and customers from the interstate highway were served in the restaurant.

States cannot impose taxes at state lines. The Import-Export Clause of the Constitution states, "no state shall, without the consent of Congress, lay any imposts or duties on imports or exports."

3.3   LIMITATIONS ON CONGRESS' POWER TO TAX

Three Limitations on Congress' Power to Tax are:

1. Direct taxes (except income tax) must be apportioned among the states.

2. All custom duties and excise taxes must be uniform throughout the U.S.

3. No duties may be levied on exports from any state.

3.4 CONGRESS' POWER TO BORROW MONEY

The Constitution of the United States delegates to Congress the power to borrow and coin money. States do not have the power to coin money, but some state constitutions allow state borrowing while other state constitutions do not allow it.

EXAMPLE

The present huge national debt certainly shows that Congress has used its Constitutional power to borrow money.

3.5 EMINENT DOMAIN

Eminent Domain is the power of government to take private property for public use upon payment of fair compensation, and this is determined by agreement or by due process of law.

3.6 THE CONTRACT CLAUSE

The Contract Clause of the Constitution mentions that no state shall pass any law impairing the obligation of contracts.

3.7 COMMERCIAL SPEECH

Commercial Speech is the Government Power to regulate Advertising. Governments may regulate or suppress commercial messages that do not accurately inform the public about lawful activity.

The Government may ban forms of communication more likely to deceive the public than to inform it, or commercial speech related to illegal activity – False Advertising.

3.8   THE DUE PROCESS CLAUSES

The Due Process Clauses of the Constitution are the Fifth and 14th Amendments.

The Fifth Amendment is that no person shall be deprived of life, liberty, or property without the due process of law.

The 14th Amendment is that no State shall deprive any person of life, liberty, or property without due process of law.

Substantive Due Process – The Supreme Court will carefully review any legislation that harms a person's freedom of speech, religion, press, peaceful assembly, and petition, the right to interstate travel, the right to vote, and the right to marry.

Procedural Due Process – In *Capital Criminal Cases*, those depriving a criminal of his or her life, the Supreme Court will review the case to be sure that the court procedures were sound.

The Supreme Court will review cases where the Government has taken away real or personal property or where the Government has dismissed an employee without fair procedure.

Equal Protection means that States cannot deny persons equal protection of the laws.

The *Rational Relationship Test of Equal Protection* means that the Supreme Court will overturn the legislation only if it is *Economic Legislation* and does not further legitimate government interest.

The *Strict Scrutiny Test* has to do with a person's *Fundamental Rights*. The Supreme Court strictly will review any law that takes away a citizen's fundamental rights.

Suspect Classifications are laws based on race or national origin.

EXAMPLE

In 1954, the desegregation case of Brown (Plaintiff) vs. Board of Education of Topeka (Defendant), the court ruled that segregated public school systems violated the Equal Protection guarantee. Since then, the Court has forbid segregated public beaches, municipal golf courses, buses, parks, and courtroom seating.

EXAMPLE (One Person, One Vote Rule)

Legislatures represent people, not trees or acres. The Legislature cannot provide that the votes of citizens in one part of the state should be given two times, or five times, or ten times the weight of votes of citizens in another part of the state.

Seats in both houses of a Bicameral State Legislature must be apportioned on a population basis. (However, this does not appear to be necessary for the United States Senate, where all states, both large and small, have two senators each.)

Equal Protection Based on Sex – Sometimes the Supreme Court grants equal protection based on sex, and sometimes not.

There must be a substantial relationship to an important Government objective before there is sexual equality.

EXAMPLE

Cases where the Court decided FOR sexual equality:

In *Orr vs. Orr*, the court allowed alimony to be given from wives to husbands, as well as from husbands to wives.

In *Reed vs. Reed*, the court allowed women to be administrators of estates as well as allowing men to be administrators.

EXAMPLE

Cases where the court decided AGAINST sexual equality:

The Supreme Court has upheld a California statutory rape law which imposed penalties only upon males.

The Supreme Court has exempted women from registering for the draft.

REVIEW QUESTIONS

1. What is the Supreme Law of the Land?
The U.S. Constitution.

2. Except for the U.S. Constitution, what is the Supreme Law of each state?
The State Constitution.

3. The Supreme Court can declare laws of Congress unconstitutional. What is the name of this power?
Judicial Review.

4. What are the three branches of government?
Executive, Legislative, and Judicial.

5. What is meant by the Separation of Powers?
Each branch of government must be allowed to function without interference from the other branches.

6. The Federal Government has limited powers. What is meant by this statement?

The Federal Government has only the powers given it by the Constitution.

7. Why is the interstate commerce clause of the Constitution so important?

It regulates business, and it also gives the federal government a chance to expand its power.

8. What is meant by the term free trade within the U.S.?

The Constitution forbids the states from imposing tariffs.

9. How do direct taxes differ from indirect taxes?

Direct taxes are imposed directly on the taxpayers – such as sales taxes and income taxes. Indirect taxes are not imposed directly on the taxpayer – such as tariffs.

10. What is eminent domain?

The power of federal, state, and local governments to take private property for public use against the will of the owner, providing that fair compensation is paid.

11. How is fair compensation determined?

By the courts.

12. Does the Government have the power to ban false advertising or misleading advertising by business?

Yes.

13. Can public golf courses discriminate against players because of race or sex?

No, but private golf courses can.

14. Can the upper house of a bicameral state legislature represent area rather than population?

No.

15. Can the upper house of the U.S. Congress represent area rather than population?

Yes.

16. Does the Supreme Court favor sexual equality under the law?

Not always.

CHAPTER 4

THE U.S. COURT SYSTEMS

4.1 THE FEDERAL COURT SYSTEM

The Federal Court System, taken as a whole, is not superior to the state courts. It is simply an independent system authorized by Article 3, Section 2 of the U.S. Constitution. However, the U.S. Supreme Court is the final controlling voice of all the state and federal courts, at least where questions of U.S. constitutional law are involved.

The U.S. Supreme Court has nine justices, nominated by the U.S. President and confirmed by the U.S. Senate. These are lifetime appointments.

— The U.S. Supreme Court is mainly an Appellate Court. Courts of appellate jurisdiction are higher courts, such as Courts of Appeals and the U.S. and State Supreme Courts. These take cases previously tried by lower courts.

— The U.S. Supreme Court has original jurisdiction under the Constitution in cases in which a state, ambassador, public minister, or consul is a party. Courts of original jurisdiction

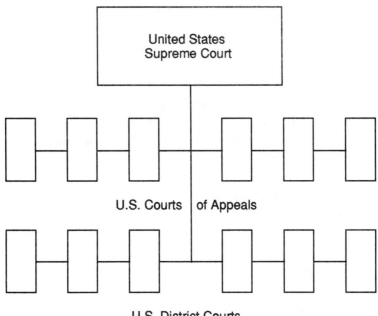

United States
Supreme Court

U.S. Courts | of Appeals

U.S. District Courts

are those that can take new cases. All courts except state and federal appellate courts have some original jurisdiction.

U.S. Courts of Appeals have appellate jurisdiction only. They hear appeals from federal district courts and also review decisions and enforcement of orders of federal administrative agencies.

U.S. District Courts have original jurisdiction over federal questions, citizenship cases, federal crimes, admiralty and maritime cases. Judges in all federal courts are appointed by the president and confirmed by the Senate.

Federal Courts with Specialized Jurisdictions are: U.S. Tax Court, U.S. Bankruptcy Court, Claims Court, Court of International Trade, Court of the Territories and Insular Possessions.

4.2 FEDERAL JURISDICTION

Which cases are tried in federal courts and which cases are left to state courts?

Federal Courts have jurisdiction over cases having to do with the United States Constitution, Laws, Treaties, or people who claim that their constitutional rights have been violated.

Federal Courts have jurisdiction over cases involving Diversity of Citizenship, that is, where citizens of different states sue each other, where citizens of a foreign country sue citizens of a state or vice versa, where the suit is for $10,000 or more. Suits of less than this can go to state courts.

EXAMPLE

Examples of Exclusive Jurisdiction by Federal Courts are federal crimes, patents, bankruptcy, copyrights.

Examples of Exclusive Jurisdiction by State Courts are cases of divorce, adoptions.

Examples of Concurrent Jurisdiction by Either Federal or State Courts are lawsuits between residents of two different states.

4.3 STATE COURT SYSTEM

A typical State Court System follows.

EXAMPLE

Examples of State Courts of Limited Jurisdiction:

1. Domestic Relations Courts (for child custody cases and divorces)

2. Local municipal courts (such as traffic courts)

3. Probate Courts (to settle wills and estates)

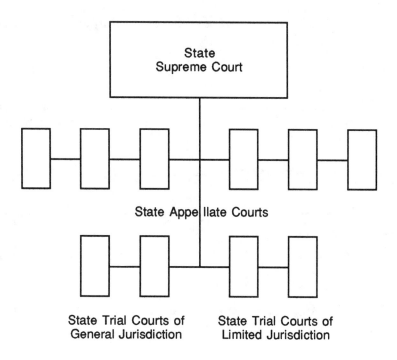

State
Supreme Court

State Appellate Courts

State Trial Courts of
General Jurisdiction

State Trial Courts of
Limited Jurisdiction

4. Small Claims Courts

5. Justice of the Peace Courts

4.4 ARBITRATION

Arbitration is becoming an increasingly popular alternative to the court system; it is less formal.

— The parties in the dispute agree in advance to abide by the arbitrator's decision. The arbitrator is a chosen expert in the field.

— Arbitration is cheaper and faster than a court trial.

— Both parties present their sides of the argument to the arbitrator who then makes a decision.

— Most states have laws encouraging arbitration in certain types of disputes.

EXAMPLE

South Carolina has a voluntary arbitration program at the Appellate Court level, to reduce time and expense. All decisions by the arbitrator are final.

REVIEW QUESTIONS

1. Is the Federal Court System, taken as a whole, superior to the state courts?
No. They are an independent system authorized by the U.S. Constitution.

2. Where U.S. constitutional law questions are involved, what is the controlling voice?
The U.S. Supreme Court.

3. How are U.S. Supreme Court justices chosen?
By the U.S. President and confirmed by the U.S. Senate

4. How are the justices of the lower federal courts chosen?
By the U.S. President and confirmed by the U.S. Senate.

5. What is meant by the term original jurisdiction?
A court with original jurisdiction takes the case first.

6. What is meant by the term appellate jurisdiction?
A court with appellate jurisdiction takes a case only if it has been tried by another court first and then appealed to this court.

7. What kind of jurisdiction do U.S. District Courts have?

Original jurisdiction over most federal cases.

8. What kind of jurisdiction do U.S. Courts of Appeals have?

Appellate jurisdiction over federal cases.

9. What kind of jurisdiction does the U.S. Supreme Court have?

Appellate jurisdiction over federal cases and original jurisdiction over cases in which a state, ambassador, public minister or consul is a party.

10. What kind of jurisdiction do the U.S. Tax Court, the U.S. Bankruptcy Court, the U.S. Court of Claims, the Court of International Trade, and the Court of the Territories and Insular Possessions have?

Original jurisdiction in their specialized areas.

11. What is Diversity of Citizenship?

Where different litigants in a case are residents of different states or different nations.

12. In what courts would divorces be tried?

In State Trial Courts of General Jurisdiction or in Domestic Relations Courts.

13. In what courts would bankruptcies be tried?

In U.S. District Courts or in the U.S. Bankruptcy Court.

14. What is arbitration?

Both parties to a case allowing an arbitrator, an expert, to make the decision.

15. Why is arbitration being used more extensively lately?

It saves time, publicity, and money.

16. Are criminal cases settled by arbitration?

No, only certain types of civil cases.

17. How does arbitration work?

Both sides agree in advance to abide by the arbitrator's decision. An expert in the field is chosen to arbitrate. He hears both sides and asks questions, then comes to a decision.

CHAPTER 5

ADMINISTRATIVE LAW

5.1   GOVERNMENT AGENCIES

Government Agencies are often labeled **"The Fourth Branch of Government."**

Agencies are set up in ever greater numbers because of the increasing complexity of the social, economic, and industrial life of the U.S.

Administrative Functions of some government agencies are national safety, welfare, military forces, police, naturalization, taxation, coining money, elections, environmental protection, consumer protection, regulation of transportation, interstate highways, labor relations, public health, safety, welfare.

Some of the more important state boards have these functions: Regulate banking, insurance, communications, transportation, public utilities, pollution, workmen's compensation.

Examples of government agencies set up by Congress are: Environmental Protection Agency, Consumer Product Safety

Commission, Equal Employment Opportunity Commission, Federal Communication Commission, Federal Deposit Insurance Corporation, Federal Reserve Board, Federal Trade Commission, Interstate Commerce Commission, National Labor Relations Board, Securities and Exchange Commission, and Small Business Administration.

5.2   OPERATIONS OF GOVERNMENT AGENCIES

Typical operations of government agencies consist of the following:

Rulemaking is a legislative power of the agency.

EXAMPLE

The Federal Communications Commission set up rules for cable television such as: Minimum of 20-channel capacity, available on a first-come, non-discriminatory basis, to furnish equipment and facilities for such access.

The purpose is to insure public access to these facilities.

Enforcement is an executive power of the agency. Congress has conferred on agencies broad investigative powers.

Adjudication is a judicial power of the agency. The agencies conduct hearings presided over by an administrative law judge.

REVIEW QUESTIONS

1. Why are government agencies often called the fourth branch of government?
Because they often act independently of the other branches of government.

2. Why have these agencies been set up?

Because our economic, industrial and social life has become so complex that more government help seems to be required by the citizens.

3. Where do these agencies get their authority?

From Congress or from the state legislatures.

4. What powers do these agencies have?

Some legislative, executive and judicial powers, but only in their narrow fields.

5. Give an example of a legislative power of a government agency.

RULEMAKING. For instance, the Federal Communications Commission can make rules regarding how cable television stations are operated.

6. Give an example of an executive power of a government agency.

ENFORCEMENT. These agencies can investigate businesses and people to see that their rules are enforced in their narrow areas of operation.

7. Give an example of a judicial power of a government agency.

ADJUDICATION. An agency can bring people before it for a hearing before an administrative law judge.

CHAPTER 6

CRIMINAL LAW

6.1   WHAT IS CRIMINAL LAW?

Criminal Law is a part of *Public Law* that is designed to prevent harm to society by declaring what conduct is criminal and establishing punishment for such conduct.

Examples of punishment for crime are fines, imprisonment, and death.

6.2   THE LAW IN CRIMINAL CASES

The Law in Criminal Cases can be explained as follows: The defendant is prosecuted by the government.

EXAMPLE

The United States vs. John Doe.

EXAMPLE

The State of Iowa vs. Mary Doe.

The accused is presumed innocent until proven guilty. The Government has the burden of proof beyond a reasonable doubt, even when a person fails to testify in his or her own defense. Some serious crimes are: *Murder, Treason,* and *Larceny.* Some business crimes are: Falsely claiming to be a medical doctor, falsely claiming to be a Certified Public Accountant, issuing new stocks and bonds without the approval of the Securities and Exchange Commission, insider trading.

In order to be guilty of a crime, in most cases, a person *must commit a wrongful act* and *have criminal intent.* What is criminal intent? It is consequences a person desires to cause as well as those consequences he knows, or should know, are virtually certain to result from his conduct.

EXAMPLE

If you desire to shoot a person, then actually do shoot that person, you have criminal intent.

Modern laws even explain Corporate Crime. Can a corporation be guilty, since it cannot have criminal intent? Modern courts hold that if employees of a corporation conduct themselves as criminals, the corporation can be fined.

6.3   TYPES OF CRIMES

There are two types of crimes:

Mala in Se – Crimes that are *bad in themselves*, such as *murder*.

Mala Prohibita – Crimes that are bad because the law says they are bad, like making a left turn on a corner where this is prohibited.

6.4   CLASSIFICATIONS OF CRIMES

There are classifications of crimes as to the Seriousness of the Offense:

Felony is a serious crime punishable by death or imprisonment in a penitentiary.

Misdemeanor is a less serious crime punishable by fine or imprisonment in a local jail.

White-Collar Crimes are embezzlement, forgery, bribery, lack of product safety, health crimes, anti-trust violations, and computer crime (such as using the computer to steal money or services or to remove personal or business information, or to tamper with information.)

6.5   OFFENSES AGAINST PERSONS

Offenses against persons are as follows:

Homicide is the unlawful taking of another's life. **Murder** is the unlawful killing of another with malice aforethought.

1. **First Degree Murder** is murder with the intent or premeditated intent to commit malice, a crime punishable by death or imprisonment for life.

2. **Second Degree Murder** is murder with no intent to kill but with conduct grossly negligent or grossly reckless.

EXAMPLE

A person drives a car down Main Street at noon at 100 miles per hour and kills people.

3. **Third Degree Murder** is unintentional killing of another during the course of a crime.

4. **Manslaughter** is unlawful killing of another without

malice aforethought. **Voluntary Manslaughter** is unintentional killing of another under extenuating circumstances, such as the defendant's heated passion provided by the victim. And usually there is not enough time between the provocation and the attack for a reasonable person to have calmed himself.

EXAMPLE

A man catches his wife in the act of adultery and gets so mad that he kills either his wife or her partner.

However, if the man takes a week to track her down and then kills her, he would be guilty of murder, not manslaughter.

Involuntary Manslaughter is causing a death due to criminal negligence.

EXAMPLE

A person knows he or she has frequent epileptic seizures, then has a seizure while driving a car and kills a person.

Rape is unlawful and nonconsensual sexual intercourse. **Statutory Rape** is unforced sexual intercourse with a minor. Legally, this is considered to be criminal rape.

Battery is unlawful touching of another.

EXAMPLE

One person punches another.

One person poisons another.

Assault is an unlawful attempt, together with the actual ability, to commit a battery; it is also threatening conduct that places the victim in reasonable fear of bodily harm.

6.6   OFFENSES AGAINST PROPERTY

Offenses against property are as follows:

Larceny is *Stealing*. The six elements of Larceny must be present for the crime to exist. They are: ***Trespassing, Taking, Carrying Away, Taking Personal Property of Another Person,*** and ***with the intent to deprive the person permanently of the goods.***

EXAMPLE

Young people take a car for a joyride, intending to return it. (This is not **larceny**, because they did not intend to deprive the owner of the car **permanently.**)

Embezzlement is the improper taking of an employer's property by an agent who, through his employment, was entrusted with receiving the money or property. In order to have embezzlement there must be a serious act of interference with the owner's rights to the property.

False Pretenses are the intentional misrepresentation of fact in order to cheat another person. The victim voluntarily transfers the property to the thief.

EXAMPLE

A person goes from door to door selling opera tickets to an opera that does not exist.

Robbery is Larceny plus the fact that the property is taken from the victim directly, or else it is taken through force or threat of force.

Aggravated Robbery is one of the following:

— Robbery with a deadly weapon.

— Robbery where the robber has the intent to kill or would kill if faced with resistance.

— Robbery that involves serious bodily injury.

— Robbery by two or more persons.

Extortion (Blackmail) is the making of threats in order to obtain money or property.

Bribery is offering property to a public official in order to influence the official's decision.

— The crime of Bribery is committed when the offer is made, whether it is accepted or not.

— **Commercial Bribery** (Bribery in business) is the use of bribery to acquire new business, obtain secret information or processes, or to obtain kickbacks.

Burglary is the breaking and entering of a home of another with the intent to commit a felony. In modern law, it does not have to be the home of another person, merely a building.

Forgery is intentional falsification of a document with intent to defraud.

EXAMPLE

Signing another person's name on a check.

Preparing a false certificate of title to a stolen car.

Bad Checks mean issuing a check with insufficient funds to cover the check.

6.7   CRIMINAL DEFENSES

Criminal Defenses are valid defenses when a person is accused in court. Even if a defendant is found to have committed a criminal act, he or she will not be convicted if the person has a valid defense.

Self-Defense is the use of Reasonable Force to protect oneself against attack.

Defense of Another Person means Reasonable Force to protect another.

Defense of Property means Reasonable Force to protect property, but not deadly force.

An Insanity Defense could mean that a person does not *understand* the nature and quality of the act or could not distinguish between right or wrong. A person found "not guilty by reason of insanity" is generally committed to a mental institution and not allowed to go free.

Infancy Defense could be raised by youths between fourteen and eighteen years of age (depending on the state) who are taken to juvenile court after they have committed a crime. This is not a criminal court.

Intoxication is a defense only if a person commits a crime while intoxicated if another person forced him to drink against his or her will. (The committing of a crime after getting intoxicated voluntarily is not a defense.)

Duress is coercion by threat of serious bodily injury.

Bill, the Defendant, tells Tom, the Plaintiff, that he, Bill, will beat him up if he does not help him rob the bank.

Mistake of Fact is when a person is induced into committing a crime by a government official.

EXAMPLE

A police officer entices another citizen to commit a robbery.

The Exclusionary Rule prohibits the introduction into the court case of illegally obtained evidence.

No Self-Incrimination Rule is that a person cannot be required to testify against himself or herself (Fifth Amendment). The person can, however, be required to stand in a lineup for identification purposes, provide a handwriting sample, or take a blood test. The Fifth Amendment does not apply to business papers, only to papers of individuals.

Due Process of Law means the right of the accused to a *Fair Trial*. Charges against the accused must be made publicly and in writing, and the accused must be given the opportunity to defend himself or herself against these charges. This means that the accused has the right to a lawyer, the right to confront and cross-examine adverse witnesses and to testify in one's own behalf if desired.

The accused also has the right to a Speedy and Public Trial by an impartial jury, to have the compulsory process of obtaining witnesses in his favor, and to have a jury trial.

REVIEW QUESTIONS

1. Is Criminal Law considered part of Public Law or Private Law?

Public law.

2. Who prosecutes the criminal in a criminal case?

The government.

3. What is criminal intent?

A desire to cause the crime.

4. How can a corporation commit a crime?

If the employees of the corporation commit the crime.

5. How can a corporation be punished?

By being fined.

6. How does a felony differ from a misdemeanor?

A felony is punishable by death or serving time in the state prison. A misdemeanor is punishable by a fine or serving time in a local jail.

7. What is a white-collar crime?

A crime where no force or forced entry exists, like forgery and bribery and computer crime.

8. How does first degree murder differ from second degree murder?

First degree murder has intent to cause serious bodily harm, while second degree murder does not have this, but only gross negligence or gross recklessness.

9. How does Manslaughter differ from Murder?

Manslaughter is unintentional.

10. How does Battery differ from Assault?

Battery is unlawfully touching another person – like beating him up. Assault is threatening to beat a person up.

11. How does embezzlement differ from stealing?

Stealing is taking another's property when you do not have the right to use it. Embezzlement is taking your employer's property when you do have the right to use it.

12. What is False Pretenses?

Selling tickets to a circus that does not exist.

13. How does Robbery differ from Larceny?

Larceny is taking another's goods, and Robbery is taking another's goods in his presence, or else through force or threat of force.

14. How does Extortion differ from Blackmail?

They are the same thing.

15. What is Commercial Bribery?

Bribery in business.

16. What is duress?

A criminal defense that the person was forced to commit a crime by force or threat of force.

17. Can a person refuse to give a handwriting sample citing the Fifth Amendment?

No.

CHAPTER 7

TORTS

7.1 DEFINITION OF TORTS

Torts are Civil Wrongs causing injury to a person, to the person's property, or to the person's economic interests.

A Tort is committed when a duty owed by one person to another is breached and thus causes injury or damage to the owner of the interest.

EXAMPLE

We owe it to people with whom we deal not to beat them up. If we do beat them up, they have the right to sue us in civil court for money damages.

A business that employs an agent to conduct its business activities is also liable for the Torts committed by its agents in the course of employment.

Tort Action is when the injured party sues to recover compensation for the damage or injury sustained as a result of the defendant's wrongful conduct. This action takes place in a *civil court*, not in a *criminal court*.

7.2   CRIMINAL TORTS

An example of a tort that is a crime would be **Assault and Battery**. For the crime, Assault and Battery, the State would take action in a criminal court. If convicted, the criminal would pay a fine to the State or go to jail or both. For the tort, Assault and Battery, the defendant, if he lost, would pay money (damages) to the plaintiff.

7.3   PUNITIVE DAMAGES

Punitive Damages are Damages (money) awarded in excess of normal compensation to punish a defendant for a serious civil wrong.

7.4   PARTIES RESPONSIBLE FOR TORTS

Parties responsible for torts are usually persons who violate the personal or property rights of others and are therefore financially responsible for the damage directly caused by the act.

Minors are not always legally responsible for their torts. The insane are not always legally responsible for their torts.

7.5   TORTS AGAINST PERSONS

Examples of torts against persons:

— **Assault and Battery**.

— **False Imprisonment**.

— **False Arrest** (Some jurisdictions will not allow victims of false arrests to sue them in court.)

— **Outrageous Conduct** inflicting Emotional Distress.

EXAMPLE

Brown (Defendant) leads a noisy mob to Smith's (Plaintiff) home and threatens to lynch Smith.

Morton (Defendant) places a rattlesnake in Henson's (Plaintiff) bed.

— **Invasion of Privacy.**

EXAMPLE

Bill (the Defendant) forces his way into Mary's (Plaintiff) hospital room; takes a picture of her, and publishes it with false statements.

— **Appropriation** is using another person's name or likeness for one's own benefit.

EXAMPLE

Bill (the Defendant) uses Jim's (Plaintiff) photograph to promote Bill's business.

— **Intrusion** is Offensive and Objectionable Invasion of Privacy.

EXAMPLE

Snyder (Defendant) enters into James' (Plaintiff) home and without authority eavesdrops into James' conversations.

— **Public Disclosure of Private Facts** can be a tort. (In order for this to be a tort, this would have to be conveyed to the General Public.)

EXAMPLE

Harold Hastings (the Defendant) places a sign in the window of his store stating that Bill Smith (the Plaintiff) will not pay his $1,000 debt to Harold Hastings.

— **False Light** is Offensive Publicity placing another in a false light.

EXAMPLE

Margaret Mary (the Defendant) lists Bill Brown's (the Plaintiff) name and/or picture in a public rogues' gallery, when Bill Brown has not committed a crime.

— **Defamation of Character** is issuing a false statement to injure a person's reputation.

EXAMPLE

Charles (the Defendant) said falsely that Homer (the Plaintiff) had committed a crime or that Homer had AIDS.

Libel is Defamation communicated by writing, television, radio, etc.

Slander is oral defamation.

Defenses Against Defamation can be used in court by the defendant.

— **Truth is a Defense.** If what you say about a person is true, that person cannot successfully sue you for defamation of character.

— **Absolute Privilege** means that if libel or slander are proved in court and a defendant can claim absolute privilege, no legal relief is available to the victim of the defamation. Persons have absolute privilege due to the offices they hold or the roles they are playing. Judges, legislators, lawyers, and witnesses, when acting in their official capacities, have Absolute Privilege.

Examples of Absolute Privilege are:

— Statements made during a judicial proceeding.

— Statements made by members of Congress on the floor of Congress.

— Statements made by executive officers while in the performance of their duties.

— Statements made between spouses when they are alone.

— **Conditional (Qualified) Privilege** is used as a defense. This means that if libel or slander are proved in court, no legal relief is available to the victim of the defamation because there is some "public interest" promoted by the communication.

Examples of Communications with Conditional Privilege are:

— To protect one's own interests, or in some cases to protect the interests of others.

— Where the publisher and the recipient have a common interest (as in writing letters of reference).

— Where the publisher is commenting against public officials without the knowledge that what they say is false. (Freedom of speech and press).

7.6   TORTS AGAINST PROPERTY

Examples of Torts Against Property are:

1. **Trespass of Real Property** is the entering or remaining on land in possession of another.

2. **Nuisance** is nontrespassory invasion of another's interest in private use of land.

EXAMPLE

Odors, smoke, dust, stream or pond pollution.

3. **Trespass of Personal Property** is unauthorized use of the personal property of another.

EXAMPLE

Jim (the Plaintiff) parks his car in front of his house, and Bill (the Defendant) pushes the car around the corner. Jim looks for his car and cannot find it immediately. Bill is liable to Jim for trespass (for damages for the inconvenience only).

4. **Conversion** is intentional destruction or use of another's personal property.

EXAMPLE

Jim (the Defendant) takes Bill's (the Plaintiff) car and sells it. Bill can sue and win the full value of the car.

5. **Interference with Contractual Relations** is intentionally causing one of the parties to a contract not to perform the contract.

EXAMPLE

Jim makes a contract to sell to Bill (the Plaintiff) his car for $5,000. Darnell (the Defendant) knows of this contract and offers to buy Jim's car for $6,000, so Jim sells his car to Darnell. Bill can sue Darnell for interference.

6. **Disparagement (Injurious Falsehood)** is publication of false statements resulting in harm to another's monetary interests.

EXAMPLE

A person issues false statements regarding who is the true owner of a car, or false statements regarding the quality of a product.

7. **Fraudulent Misrepresentation** is making a false statement with knowledge of its falsity and intent to mislead.

EXAMPLE

Jim (the Defendant) tells John (the Plaintiff) that a tract of land in Oklahoma is located in an area where drilling for oil had recently commenced. This is false. But this statement induces John to buy the land.

7.7   DEFENSES AGAINST TORTS

Defenses against torts are used by defendants to win the case.

1. **Consent** is a defense because if a person consents, there is usually no liability.

EXAMPLE

Bill (the Defendant) says he wants to kiss Mary (the Plaintiff). She says nothing. He kisses her. She cannot later win a tort suit against him for battery because by doing nothing she has impliedly consented.

Consent to participate in a game is a defense.

EXAMPLE

Let us say that Harry (the Plaintiff) agrees to play baseball. He impliedly consents to the physical contact of the game. But he does not consent to getting hit over the head with a baseball bat.

Consent to a criminal act can sometimes be a legal defense.

EXAMPLE

A statute makes it a crime to sell drinks to an intoxicated person. Bill (the Defendant) sells liquor to Mike (the Plaintiff) who is intoxicated. Mike consumes the liquor and suffers physical injury from it. Mike can sue Bill for damages.

2. **Privilege** is the ability to protect oneself and to injure another person without that person's consent.

Self-Defense can mean that if there is not time to call the law, a person is allowed to use reasonable force to protect oneself against threatened harmful or offensive contact or confinement.

EXAMPLE

One may stand his ground and use deadly force if the attack occurs in his own residence, even though a reasonable means of escape exists.

Defense of Others can mean that a person may defend third persons from harmful or offensive contact just as the person can protect oneself.

Bill (the Defendant) sees Hugh (the Plaintiff) about to strike Bill's friend, Jim. Before Bill arrived on the scene, Jim started the fight with Hugh. So Hugh has the privilege to repel Jim's attack. Bill has no reason to suspect that Jim is the aggressor and intercedes to assist Jim. Bill is privileged to use reasonable force to assist Jim against Hugh.

3. **Defense of Property** – An owner of property may use reasonable force, not intended or likely to cause death or serious bodily harm, to protect his real or personal property. This is true only if the owner reasonably believes that the intrusion can be ended only by the use of force and the intruder has disregarded requests to cease.

EXAMPLE

A person may not usually use spring guns, electrified fences, and other traps that are intended or likely to cause death or serious bodily harm.

REVIEW QUESTIONS

1. If a person commits a crime, such as beating another person up, why is this taken to civil court instead of criminal court?

This beating a person up is both a crime and a tort. The crime can certainly be taken to criminal court, but the result is that if a person is convicted, he will either go to jail or pay a fine to the state. The victim will get nothing. If the victim wants money damages, he must have a tort suit in civil court.

2. Why are businesspeople interested in tort law?

Because a businessperson is liable for the torts of his agents.

3. What are punitive damages?

Extra damages in punishment for a civil wrong. Let us say that I get beaten up by Joe, and my hospital bill is $1000. I take the court suit to civil court which awards me $1000 regular damages and $500 punitive damages.

4. Are all persons responsible for the torts they commit?

No, the very young and the insane are not always responsible.

5. If a police officer thinks you are someone else and falsely imprisons you, can you sue the city?

No. Some governments will not allow you to sue them and collect anything. Also the police officer made an honest mistake in the performance of his duty so this is a valid defense by the city.

6. Doesn't libel conflict with the constitutional freedom of the press?

Yes. Newspapers and magazines have a great deal of freedom to write and publish. In order to prove libel, a person must prove malicious falsehood.

7. Give an example of conditional privilege.

A student asks a teacher to write a job recommendation for him and put it in his employment file. In the recommendation the teacher mentions that the student is often late for class. The student looks in the file and sues the teacher. As a defense the teacher may claim conditional privilege.

CHAPTER 8

CONTRACTS

8.1 DEFINITION OF CONTRACTS

Contracts are agreements which create legal obligations and are enforceable in a court of law. There are four Essentials of a Contract:

— **Mutual Assent** means that both parties must agree to the contract.

— **Consideration** means that both parties must do or pay something stated in the contract.

— **Legality of Object** means that the carrying out of a contract cannot force the parties to do something illegal; for instance, they cannot be required to burn down a building or to shoot someone.

— **Capacity of the Parties** means that all parties to the contract must have the legal ability to perform their part of the contract.

Examples of parties able to extricate themselves from contracts legally are:

— **Minors** (persons under legal age) can get out of most contracts that they make before reaching legal age. If they reach legal age, they are usually held to the contract and have only a reasonable time (usually a few months) after reaching legal age to disaffirm the contract. Minors cannot avoid contracts for necessities and cannot avoid a contract to enlist in the armed forces.

— People of unsound mind

— Drugged persons

— Intoxicated persons

Other important definitions:

Executed Contracts are those that have been carried out by all parties to the contract.

Executory Contracts are those where not all the terms of the contract have yet been carried out by all parties.

8.2   THE STATUTE OF FRAUDS

The Statute of Frauds is an ancient English law stating that certain contracts must be in writing to be legally binding:

1. The sale of real property (land, or buildings attached to the land) must be in writing to be enforceable.

2. Contracts that cannot be completely performed within a year must be in writing.

EXAMPLE

Brown (Plaintiff) sues Harland Glass Company (Defendant) on

an oral employment contract entered into in March that was to begin on May 1 of that year and end on April 30 of the following year. The court held for the Defendant because the contract was not performable within one year from the making (March) and so was unenforceable because of the Statute of Frauds.

3. The promise to pay the debt of another must be in writing (Contract of Guaranty).

4. Promises made in consideration of marriage must be in writing.

EXAMPLE

Harriet (the Defendant) tells John's mother (the Plaintiff) that if John marries her, she (Harriet) will give John's mother a new washing machine. John marries Harriet. John's mother cannot enforce the contract unless it is in writing.

5. To be personally liable for debt of an estate of someone who has died, the contract must be in writing to be enforceable.

6. The sale of goods of $500 or more must be written to be enforceable. The *Whole Contract* need not be written, but there must be at least a written memorandum for it to be legally binding.

Modification of a Written Contract must also be in writing to be enforceable in court. (If the Statute of Frauds requires a contract to be written, it can only be changed by another written contract.)

8.3   THE PAROLE EVIDENCE RULE

The Parole Evidence Rule states that when a contract is in writing, prior oral or written agreements are usually not allowed to change the terms of the contract.

EXAMPLE

Before Nancy Songer (the Plainitff) left the United States to visit the Island of Ponape, she took out medical insurance from the Continental Life & Accident Company (Defendant). She told the agent she had an "innocent" heart murmur. Arrangements were made for her to have a medical exam. The agent orally assured Nancy Songer that there was a "binder" and that she was immediately covered unless and until she heard otherwise from the company. The express written terms of the health insurance application filled out by Nancy Songer stated, "the insurance applied for will not become effective until this application has been accepted by the company at its home office." Nancy Songer signed the completed application and gave the Continental agent a check for $133 for the first six months' premium and received a receipt signed by the agent.

The agent testified that he did not tell Nancy Songer that there was immediate coverage, but instead explained to her that coverage would begin as of the date of application if the application was later accepted by the company.

Sixty days later, on Ponape, Nancy was involved in an auto accident. A few days later, Continental gave written notice that the application for medical insurance was being declined for medical and other reasons. Accompanying the notice was a refund check from Continental. Nancy Songer never endorsed the check or accepted the refund.

The Court decided in favor of the Continental Insurance Company because of the Parole Evidence Rule. This rule provides that "in the absence of fraud or mistake, Parole Evidence is inadmissible to change, alter or vary the express terms of the written contract."

8.4 BREACH OF CONTRACT

Breach of Contract is the failure of one or more parties to comply with the terms of the contract.

Mary Smith (Plaintiff) agrees to sell 40,000 pounds of plastic resin to Don Brittain, free on board Brittain's factory, delivery by March 1. On February 1, Brittain wrongfully repudiates the contract by telephoning Smith and telling her that he does not want the resin. Mary Smith immediately seeks another buyer, but before she is able to locate one, and within a reasonable time, the resin is destroyed by a fire through no fault of Mary Smith. The fair market value of the resin is $35,000. Mary Smith's insurance covers only $15,000 of the loss. Don Brittain is liable for $20,000.

8.5   NOVATION

In a contract between three people, a **novation** means substituting a new party for an old one.

EXAMPLE

Bowen owes Arthur $500. Arthur, Bowen, and Cameron agree that Cameron will pay the debt and that Bowen will be discharged. The novation is the substitution of the new debtor, Cameron, for the old debtor, Bowen.

8.6   ACCORD AND SATISFACTION

Accord and Satisfaction is the legal term meaning that the Duties of the contract are later changed, with the consent of all the parties.

EXAMPLE

John owes Bill $500 under the contract. This John cannot pay. So both parties agree to let John paint Bill's house. This is the **accord**. When John actually paints Bill's house, this is the **satisfaction**, which discharges the debt.

8.7   UNILATERAL AND BILATERAL CONTRACTS

A Unilateral Contract is a promise for an act or a forbearance to act. (**Forbearance** means a promise not to do something that legally one could do.) Unilateral Contracts are "when only one party makes a promise." This type of contract is formed only when the second party has done what the contract calls for.

EXAMPLE

James (the Defendant) promises Miller (the Plaintiff) that if Miller paints his (James') house, James will pay Miller $500. Miller paints the house, so the $500 is due Miller.

A Bilateral Contract is where the first party makes an offer and the second party accepts it.

EXAMPLE

Armour (the Plaintiff) says to Bishop (the Defendant), "If you promise to mow my lawn, I will give you $10." Then Bishop agrees to mow Armour's lawn. These are mutual promises.

8.8   CONSIDERATION AND PAST CONSIDERATION

Consideration is the **Benefit** that a person gets from a contract or the *price paid* by the contracting party. It is some right, interest, or profit accruing to one party, or some forbearance, detriment, loss or responsibility given or undertaken by the other party.

Past Consideration means work done or money given *prior* to the signing of the contract. Past Consideration is legally *No Consideration.*

EXAMPLE

Mary (the Plaintiff) took care of John's adult incapacitated son for six months. John told Mary that he would pay her $500 for this past care. John cannot be held to this.

8.9   ADEQUACY OF CONSIDERATION

Adequacy of Consideration is not important in a contract. As long as there is any consideration at all, that is enough to make the contract legally enforceable.

EXAMPLE

John (the Defendant) gives Mary (the Plaintiff) $1 for taking care of his lawn. There is consideration, though perhaps not adequate, and that makes it a legally binding contract.

8.10   INTERPRETATION OF CONTRACTS

Interpretation of Contracts means rules set up by the courts in the past to look at contracts to see whether or not they are legally binding.

Contracts are interpreted to follow the Intention of the Parties as expressed in the contract.

Interpretation as a whole means that the entire contract must be looked at. Important provisions in fine print are generally not enforceable.

Party Causing Uncertainty means that the contract language should be interpreted most strongly against the party who caused the uncertainty to exist. That is, the one who wrote the contract.

Insurance Contracts are usually interpreted against the insurance company, because usually the insurance company writes the contract.

If one party is in one state and another party is in another state, which law does a court use to interpret the contract? The law in the location where the Acceptor to the contract lives. The Offeror starts the contract negotiations and the Acceptor agrees, making the contract enforceable.

8.11   A QUASI-CONTRACT

A Quasi-Contract is an Implied-In-Fact Contract, so is really no contract at all. No Express or Implied Promise is made. It is imposed by law in order to assure that a just and equitable result will occur.

EXAMPLE

Bill (the Plaintiff) by mistake delivers to Robert (the Defendant) a plain, unaddressed envelope containing $1,000 intended for Claudia. Robert is under no contractual obligation to return it. However, Bill is permitted to recover the $1,000 from Robert. The law imposes an obligation upon Robert in order to prevent his unjust enrichment at the expense of Bill.

REVIEW QUESTIONS

1. What are Contracts?

Legally enforceable agreements.

2. If a woman agrees to go on a date with a man, is that a contract?

No. It is an agreement but is not legally enforceable. If the woman "stood the man up," he could not win a lawsuit against her. It is merely a social agreement.

3. What is Consideration in a contract?

Both parties must be obliged to do something in the contract before it is legally enforceable.

4. What is meant by capacity?

Being legally obligated to carry out the contract. That is, being of legal age and of sound mind.

5. What is the Statute of Frauds?

An English law stating what types of contracts must be in writing to be legally enforceable.

6. Does the Statute of Frauds say the whole contract must be written?

No, but there must be at least a written memorandum to make it legally binding.

7. What is the important part of the Parole Evidence Rule?

If a contract is in writing, any extra oral terms are usually not enforceable.

8. What is meant by the term breach of contract?

One or more parties to the contract fails to carry out the terms of the contract.

9. What is Novation?

After the contract is made, all the other parties to the contract agree to substitute a new party for one of the old parties to the contract.

10. What is Accord and Satisfaction?

After the contract is made, all parties to the contract agree to change one or more of the terms of the contract.

11. What is the difference between an executed contract and an executory contract?

In an executed contract all the terms of the contract have been carried out by the parties to the contract. In an executory contract, not all the terms of the contract have yet been carried out.

12. What is a bilateral contract?

Both parties to the contract have duties before the contract can be carried out.

13. What is a unilateral contract?

One where only one party makes a promise. The second party accepts the contract only when he or she carries out the terms of the contract completely.

14. What is consideration?

Doing whatever the party is supposed to do under the contract. The benefit a party receives or the price a party pays under the contract is the consideration. For a contract to be valid, there must be consideration on the part of both parties.

15. What is past consideration?

Something that one of the parties did prior to the time the contract was made.

16. Why is past consideration no consideration?

Parties to a contract must use present consideration in order to make the contract legally enforceable. That is, they must do something – that which is stated in the contract, after the contract has been agreed upon.

17. What is adequacy of consideration?

This is the idea that each party must do a great deal in the contract. It is of no validity. In determining whether or not a contract is enforceable, the court will merely determine whether or not there has been consideration on the part of both parties to the contract. Adequacy of consideration is not weighed.

18. When a court is interpreting a contract, which is more important – the intention of the parties as expressed in the contract, or the intention of the parties as expressed or implied outside the contract?
The intention of the parties as expressed in the contract.

19. Which is more important, the main contract or the fine print?
The main contract.

20. If there is a conflict between the parties to the contract on the wording of the contract, who should be favored by the court?
The person who did not write the contract.

21. If parts of the contract disagree, which is more important – the printed part of the contract or the unprinted part of the contract?
The unprinted part of the contract.

22. If there is a conflict between an insurance company and a policyholder regarding the terms of the contract, which party should have the most burden of proof?
The insurance company.

23. Is a Quasi-Contract a contract?
No.

24. If a Quasi-Contract is not a contract, why does the law allow it?
To assure a just and equitable result.

CHAPTER 9

AGENCY

9.1 DEFINITION OF AGENCY

Agency is assigning someone else to do something for us. (The Assignor is the Principal, and the Assignee is the Agent.)

Examples of Agency:

— We appoint a licensed real estate broker to act as our agent in the sale of eighty acres of farmland.

— We let someone use our car to drive the children to school, and this driver is our agent.

Legal business activities can be assigned to an agent.

Illegal Activities, such as burning down a building, or *Personal Services*, such as a painter painting a picture, cannot be assigned to an agent.

9.2 EMPLOYER-EMPLOYEE RELATIONS

In Employer-Employee Relations the Employer can *control* the acts of the employee (Example: a full-time chauffeur), and the employer is usually liable for the employee's torts.

9.3   INDEPENDENT CONTRACTOR RELATIONS

In Independent Contractor Relations, the Contractor cannot control the acts of the other party in the contract, the independent contractor. (Example: Taxi Driver). He has contracted for a specific job only. The contractor is not usually liable for the torts of an independent contractor.

9.4   AGENCY CONTRACTS

Agency Contracts may be written or oral, and do not require consideration.

Agency Contracts which must be written are: Giving the agent authority to buy or sell land for the principal, and appointment of the agent for more than one year.

A Power of Attorney is the written, formal appointment of an agent.

The Capacity to be a Principal is determined by one being of age and not insane.

In the determination of Capacity to be an Agent, some minors, if not extremely young, can be agents. Incompetents not under a guardianship may be agents in some cases.

9.5   DUTIES OF AGENT TO PRINCIPAL

Obedience — If a principal tells an agent not to sell on credit and the agent does sell on credit, the agent is liable to the principal for the amount of the loss.

Diligence — If the principal tells the agent to sell in a high nearby market, and the agent sells in a low market, the agent is liable to the principal.

Inform — When an agent finds out that a customer is bankrupt, the agent has the duty to inform the principal of this fact.

Account — Agent must account to principal for goods and monies. Agent must keep the principal's goods and property and money separate from his own.

Fiduciary — There must be the utmost loyalty and good faith on the part of the agent to the principal. An agent cannot compete against the principal, the agent cannot make a secret profit from his or her agency.

9.6 DUTIES OF PRINCIPAL TO AGENT

Contractual Duties — Principal must *compensate* the agent for the agent's work. (If no compensation has been agreed upon, a *reasonable compensation* is necessary, unless the agent has agreed to serve free of charge.)

Accounting — The principal must give the agent a true accounting.

Reimbursement — If the agent pays the fire insurance premium for the principal, the agent must be reimbursed by the principal.

Indemnification — The principal must repay the agent for losses that the agent incurs in the process of agency work.

Tort Duties — The principal must provide the agent with a safe workplace. The principal is liable for the employees' injuries on the job.

9.7   TERMINATION OF AGENCY

Termination of Agency comes about by *Lapse of Time, Mutual Agreement of Parties, Fulfillment of Purpose, Revocation of Agent's Authority by the Principal; Renunciation of the Contract by the Agent, Death of Either the Principal or the Agent,* and *Bankruptcy.*

Incapacity is when the agent or principal goes insane.

Change in Business Conditions can terminate the agency. An agent is authorized by the principal to sell a piece of land for $1500. Then oil is discovered. This terminates the agent's right to sell the land for $1500.

Loss or Destruction of Subject Matter could end the agent's contract.

Loss of Qualification of Principal or Agent might end the contract. (The principal loses his state liquor license so the agent can no longer work in the package store owned by the principal.)

Disloyalty of Agent ends agency.

Change of Law could end agency contract. The agent works in the principal's liquor store. The state becomes dry and prohibition sets in. This cancels the agency.

Outbreak of War ends agency sometimes. Brown is our agent to sell our cars in Germany. War breaks out between the U.S. and Germany. The agency contract is broken.

9.8   LABOR LAW

Labor Law is extremely important to businesspeople today. Some of the more important labor laws follow:

Norris-LaGuardia Act of 1932 provided that federal courts cannot issue injunctions in non-violent labor disputes. Labor has the full freedom to form labor unions without interference by the employer.

An injunction is a Court Order of Equity to refrain from doing or to do a specified act (such as to stop tearing up a street with a bulldozer). Its use in labor disputes has been greatly restricted by recent laws.

National Labor Relations Act of 1935 mentioned that Labor has the legal right to *Bargain Collectively* with management.

Collective Bargaining is the process by which the terms of employment are agreed upon through negotiations between the employer or employers within a given industry or industrial area and the union or the bargaining representative of the employees.

Management is not allowed to dominate the union, to discriminate against union members, and management must bargain in good faith with duly established representatives of the employees. This law set up the National Labor Relations Board to supervise elections of unions and to monitor employee rights.

Taft-Hartley Act of 1947 forbade secondary boycotts. However, recent law has somewhat changed this.

Primary Boycotts are the concerted refusal by labor to handle the products of an employer against whom they are striking. This is legal.

Secondary Boycotts are concerted coercive action aimed at a neutral employer, one that is not targeted in the labor dispute, but one who deals with the targeted employer. This is usually illegal under the Taft-Hartley Act.

Three Exceptions where secondary boycotts could be legal:

1. **Ally Doctrine** — If, during a strike, the main employer subcontracts work to another in order to evade the effects of the strike, the union may legally strike or picket the subcontractor.

2. **Common Situs Picketing** — In construction projects many employer subcontractors work side by side. Where one subcontractor has a labor dispute with its employees, primary and secondary employers are working side by side. A primary picket also inadvertently pickets other employers, which is really legal picketing, although secondary.

3. **Product Picketing** —A Fruit and Vegetable Packers Union protests the practice of Washington State apple growers in not using union labor to pick and pack their apples. So the union pickets the orchards. This is Primary Picketing, Primary Boycott — and legal. The union also pickets Safeway Stores, asking customers not to purchase Washington State apples. This is legal, because the store handles many other products, and the picketing was not attempting to shut off customers from buying other products.

The **Taft-Hartley Act** also forbid jurisdictional strikes over

80

work assignments, refusing to bargain in good faith, feather-bedding (*Featherbedding* is the unions forcing employers to continue jobs no longer needed, such as firemen on the rail-roads) and to force an employer to discharge or discriminate against nonunion employees. An employer was allowed to give statements and opinions as long as they contained no threat of reprisal. The act reinstated the availability of civil injunctions in labor disputes, but only against an unfair labor practice and at the request of the National Labor Relations Board.

Landrum-Griffin Act of 1959 attempted to eliminate cor-ruption in labor unions and tried to make unions more demo-cratic. An elaborate union reporting system was installed to be sure that union members could attend meetings, have free ex-pression and fair hearings before a union could take action against them.

Civil Rights Act of 1964 prohibited discrimination in em-ployment based on race, sex, religion, or national origin.

Equal Pay Act provided that employers cannot discrimi-nate between employees on the basis of sex by paying unequal wages for the same work.

Equal Employment Opportunity Commission was set up by the Civil Rights Act to attempt to resolve alleged viola-tions, to investigate charges of discrimination, to issue guide-lines and regulations.

Basic Defenses of Employers under the Civil Rights Act are:

— The employing company has a "good faith" Seniority or Merit System for its employees.

— The employing company has a professionally developed *Ability Test*, to be administered to its employees.

— The employing company has a "Good Faith" set of Occupational Qualifications that it uses in hiring, transferring, and promoting employees.

Affirmative Action is active recruitment of minority applicants.

Age Discrimination in Employment Act of 1967 prohibits discriminating in hiring, firing, salaries, or otherwise on the basis of age. It is especially concerned with employees aged 40 through 70 years.

Rehabilitation Act of 1973 helped the handicapped in obtaining rehabilitation training, access to public facilities, and employment. Federal contractors and agencies must take affirmative action in hiring the handicapped.

Occupational Safety and Health Act of 1970 was set up to assure a safe and healthful working environment.

— The Occupational Safety and Health Administration develops standards, conducts inspections, monitors compliance, and institutes enforcement actions against those not in compliance.

— The act prohibits employers from discharging or discriminating against an employee who exercises his or her rights under the act.

Fair Labor Standards Act protects working children and youth. It prohibits the employment of child labor outside of agriculture. It allows no employment of anyone under age 14 except as newspaper deliverers and as child actors. Fourteen- and fifteen-year-olds may be employed outside school hours in certain nonhazardous jobs. Sixteen-year-olds and seventeen-year-olds may work at *any non-hazardous job*. Persons eighteen years old or older may work at any job. The law sets a minimum wage and sets overtime pay of time-and-a-half for working over 40 hours per week.

Social Security Act of 1935 sets up federal retirement and death benefits, survivors' insurance, disability insurance, hospitalization insurance (Medicare), Supplemental Security Income, and unemployment insurance.

REVIEW QUESTIONS

1. What is an agent?

A person whom we assign to do something for us.

2. Can we assign any job to an agent?

No. Illegal activities cannot be assigned, such as killing someone. Neither can we assign extremely personal activities. For instance, we have been assigned to play the church organ. We cannot assign this to another person who may not be so skilled, without permission from some higher authority.

3. How does an Independent Contractor differ from an Employee?

The employer can control the actions of an employee and therefore is responsible for his torts. On the other hand, an independent contractor's actions are not under the control of the other contractor so the other contractor is not responsible for his torts.

4. Do agency contracts require consideration in order to be legally binding?

No.

5. What is the name of a written, formal appointment of an agent?

Power of Attorney.

6. What is meant by the term capacity?

The legal right to enter into a contract. This has to do with a person's age and mental stability.

7. What is an injunction?

A court order to cease doing something. This is usually temporary.

8. What act forbid federal courts from issuing injunctions in a peaceful labor dispute?

Norris-LaGuardia Act of 1932.

9. What is Collective Bargaining?

The right of representatives of a union to sit down at a table with Management and come to a binding labor agreement representing all employees.

10. What is a primary boycott?

Strikers refuse to buy the products made by their employer.

11. What is a secondary boycott?

Persons favoring the strikers refuse to buy the products made by the employer of the strikers.

12. What is featherbedding?

Forcing the employer to hire people doing unneeded work. (Hiring firemen on modern gasoline railroad engines.)

CHAPTER 10

SALES

10.1 DEFINITION OF A SALE

A Sale is a contract in which ownership of goods passes immediately from the seller to the buyer for a price.

EXAMPLE

While shopping at an appliance store, the Smiths (Defendants) signed a contract agreeing to buy a television set when the new models arrived in ten days. (This is not a sale. It is a contract to sell, because the ownership of the goods is to transfer in the future.) However, this contract to sell is governed by the law of sales in the Uniform Commercial Code.

Barter is a type of sale where goods are exchanged for goods, without money.

The Uniform Commercial Code is a law giving uniform business rules which have been adopted by all states except Louisiana. With the growth of business and the speed of transportation, greater uniformity of laws governing business and commercial transactions has become a necessity. Part of the Uniform Code deals with *Sales*.

Goods are items of tangible, movable personal property.

Tangible Property is property which can be touched and used, like a car or grain. (On the other hand, *Intangible Property* would be stocks, bonds, patents, and copyrights. The paper on which they are written can be touched, but the property or value itself cannot really be touched.)

Personal Property is movable items not attached to the land, such as trailers, cars, boats, clothing, and furniture.

Fungible Goods are goods or securities of which any unit is, by nature or usage of trade, the equivalent of any other like unit. (Oil, corn, flour, wheat, cotton, sugar, canned goods.)

A Merchant is a seller who deals regularly in a particular kind of goods or claims to have special knowledge or skill in a certain type of sales transaction.

A Casual Seller is anyone who sells only occasionally.

10.2   SALES OF PERSONAL PROPERTY

The Uniform Commercial Code states that sales apply only to the sale of movable personal property, tangible property. (Food, vehicles, clothing, furniture.)

Price is money or money's worth. It may be payable in *Money, Goods,* or *Services*.

Contracts To Sell are promises to buy or sell in the future.

Sale of Goods vs. Contract for Services — If the most important part of the contract is Services (like hiring a plumber who may also install a washer), then it is a *Contract for Services*, and not a *Sale*.

Goods in the sales contract must be *Existing Goods*. In order for the sale to be valid, the goods must be in existence at the time of the agreement (not future fish to be caught) and they must be owned by the seller (vendor).

A *Bill of Sale* is written evidence of one's title to tangible personal property. It is not required to have a Bill of Sale but it is good to have in case of disagreement.

10.3   THE FORMALITIES OF A SALE

A sale of $500 or more must be in writing; otherwise a sale can be oral, written, or implied from conduct.

Receipt and Acceptance by the buyer is required in a valid sale. **Receipt** is taking possession of the goods; **Acceptance** is the assent of the buyer to become the owner of the goods.

No Writing Is Required, even if the sale is over $500, if there is *Receipt and Acceptance*, or *Judicial Admission*. (*Judicial Admission* is when a person admits in court that a sales contract was made, or if the sale was of *Non-Sellable Goods*. Non-sellable goods are goods made specifically for that person.)

Auction Sales are oral and legal, even if over $500.

10.4   TRANSFER OF TITLE

An owner may dispose of property by transferring it to another. This can be done by sale (for a price) or by gift (freely given without payment) or by will at death, or if there is no will, by virtue of state statutes of inheritance.

Creditors' Claims must be taken into account. Creditors of the buyer or of the seller may claim the television set if they can prove that their debtor owns the set.

Terms of the Transaction are important. Title passes when the terms of the transaction have been carried out.

Damage to Unidentified Goods has special rules. So long as the goods are not specifically set aside, no risk of loss has passed to the buyer.

Sale on Approval means that title and risk of loss remain with the seller until the lapse of a reasonable time or until the buyer acts in a manner that is not consistent with a reasonable trial.

Sale or Return means that title and risk of loss pass to the buyer immediately.

Sale on Consignment is no real sale at all. It merely means that the property is in the possession of the consignee for sale. The consignor may retake possession of the property at will. (*Consignment* means a dealer has *Possession* of the property but not *Ownership*.)

Sales of Fungible Goods (like wheat in a bin) have different rules. For instance, sale of only part of the wheat in a bin may pass from the seller to the buyer at the time of the transaction, making the buyer an owner in common with the seller, since after the sale part of the wheat in the bin will be owned by the buyer and part by the seller.

Free on Board means that if the contract calls for goods to be sold *Free on Board* at a designated point, the seller bears the risk and expense until the goods are delivered to the point designated, then the buyer assumes risk and expense.

C.O.D. means that the carrier is not to deliver the goods to the buyer until the buyer pays the carrier. This has no effect on when title or risk passes.

Legal Transfer of Title depends on circumstances. People can transfer or sell only such interest or title as that which they possess. (If you buy a car from a thief, you do not own the car.)

Sale by Entrustee is possible. An **Entrustee** is a person to whom you entrust your property. For instance, if we leave your watch with a jeweler to be fixed, and if the jeweler then sells the watch to someone else, the title passes. But then, of course, the jeweler is liable to the person who left the watch.

Consignment Sales have special rules. If a dealer has a regular place of business and sells goods on consignment, the creditors of the dealer may reach the goods as though they were owned by the dealer.

Documents of Title are Bills of Lading and Warehouse Receipts. They have a certain degree of **Negotiability**. (Negotiability is the ability to pass title in a business transaction.) The holder of these bills may transfer to a purchaser acting in good faith the title to the property.

Recording and Filing Statutes are important to sellers and buyers. Some states require that if goods are sold on credit, the seller must file a financing statement at a government office — often at the courthouse. If the seller fails to do so, and the purchaser sells the goods to an innocent third party, the innocent third party receives title to the goods.

Voidable Title means that in certain instances, the owner may lose his title to the goods. Here is an example: If the buyer of the goods has obtained the goods by fraud (bad check, larceny, or trick), and sells the goods to an innocent third party, the innocent third party gets title to the goods.

10.5 WARRANTIES

Warranties are guarantees.

An **Express Warranty** is a guarantee that the article will conform to a certain standard or operate in a certain manner. If this is made by the seller to the buyer, it becomes part of the sales contract.

Seller's Opinion is not a guarantee. "The best on the market" or "They are worth $5 if they are worth a dime." These opinions do not constitute warranties.

Apparent Defects are defects known to the buyer, or defects so apparent that no special skill is required to detect them. These are not covered by warranties.

Warranties of all sellers are:

1. **Warranty of Title** means that the Buyer assumes that the Seller has title. (Exceptions are Sheriff, Auctioneer, or Administrator.)

2. **Warranty Against Encumbrances** means that there are no liens on the property to be sold. (A *Lien* is a legal claim of one person upon the property of another person to secure the payment of a debt or the satisfaction of an obligation.)

3. **Warranty of Conformity to Description, Sample, or Model** is also a form of guarantee. (A *Sample* is a portion of a whole mass, and a *Model* is a replica of the article in question.)

4. An example of a **Warranty of Fitness for a Particular Purpose** follows: If the seller knows that a buyer wants the goods for some particular and unusual purpose, the seller may make an implied warranty that the goods will fit that purpose.

EXAMPLE

The Buyer wants a tape that will fit a certain computer system.

Additional Warranties of a **Merchant Seller** follow: (A *Merchant Seller* is one who normally engages in certain sales and who thus should have particular knowledge or skill.)

1. **Warranty Against Infringement** means that the goods are free of claims by a third party regarding patent or copyright infringement.

2. An example of a **Warranty of Fitness For Normal Use** Follows: Candy Machine is guaranteed to make candy.

Examples of a **Warranty In Particular Sales:**

1. **Sale of Food or Drink**: Warranty that it is fit for human consumption.

2. **Sale of Article with Patent or Trade Name** means that it is fit for a particular purpose if the buyer relied on the seller's skill and judgment.

3. In a **Sale on Buyer's Specification**, regular warranties arise, but no warranty of fitness for a particular purpose can arise.

4. In a **Sale of Secondhand Or Used Goods,** there is no warranty by a casual seller. If made by a Merchant Seller,

some warranty may exist, especially if made in the sale of used automobiles and equipment.

5. **Full Warranties** are written for a consumer product.

They guarantee that the seller will remedy any defects that the buyer finds in the product in a reasonable time after sale, without charge.

They permit the purchaser to choose a refund or replacement without charge if the product contains a defect after a reasonable number of attempts by the warrantor to remedy the defects.

Caveat Emptor means *Let the Buyer Beware*. If there is no fraud or warranty in the sale, the buyer is usually the loser.

Product Liability means that the maker is responsible if his products harm the person or property of the buyer.

EXAMPLE

Children's Toys Catch Fire.

— **Negligence** means that a person injured through the use or condition of the personal property that the person bought may be entitled to sue the manufacturer for damages.

— **Manufacturer of a Component Part** could be liable. In some jurisdictions the manufacturer of a component part can be successfully sued by a person hurt by the machine.

EXAMPLE

A car rolls downhill and hits a pedestrian. The pedestrian can sue the company that made the defective brake. (In this case the pedestrian is the Plaintiff and the company is the Defendant.)

10.6 CONSUMER PROTECTION

Usury Laws forbid charging excessive interest on loans. Most states have a *Legal Rate of Interest* for loans, usually from 5% to 15% for loans where no interest rate has been specified. The *Legal Contract Rate* varies from 8% to 45%, depending on the state. States usually allow an even higher interest rate than this on small loans. Rates higher than these legal rates are usurious and therefore illegal.

Antitrust Laws prevent companies from merging if they control too much of the market for that product. (The Government fears that monopolistic companies will charge prices that are too high.)

Product Safety is stressed in today's laws.

EXAMPLE

Examples of products where laws require product safety: Bumpers, Tires, Auto Glass, Toys, Television Sets, Insecticides, Drugs.

Consumer Product Safety Commission was set up by the Consumer Product Safety Act of 1982. It sets safety standards for many products and can ban inherently dangerous or hazardous products.

Truth in Advertising is law today. The Federal Trade Commission can demand that false or deceptive advertising be stopped.

Truth in Lending Act states that lenders must give the exact yearly interest rate and the total finance charge in a sale or sales contract. When a person finances the purchase of consumer products through a mortgage on his principal dwelling, the person has three days to back out.

Product Uniformity laws are now important. Some states require that some products be packaged in specifically comparable quantities so that customers can make intelligent choices between competing products.

1. Some states require that packaged products show the price per ounce or per pound.

2. The Federal Government requires sellers of autos to publish mileage test data in marketing new cars.

Warranty Act (Magnuson-Moss Warranty and Federal Trade Commission Improvement Act of 1975) provides:

1. Clear understandable disclosure of all warranties must be made.

2. Legal remedies of the consumer must be clearly stated.

3. The consumer must be informed of the warranty prior to the sale.

4. The consumer is allowed an extension of warranty time if the repairs require that the product be out of service for an unreasonable length of time.

EXAMPLE

Brown (the Plaintiff) bought a lawn mower with WARRANTY OF REPAIRS GUARANTEED for one year. After seven months Brown took the mower to the seller (the Defendant) for necessary repairs. The seller retained the mower for six months in making the repairs. Brown's Warranty is extended.

Fair Credit Reporting Act specifies that:

1. Creditors must notify a potential recipient of credit when-

ever they deny credit based on a credit report.

2. Debtors can go to the credit agency and look up the credit report in their personal file.

3. If the credit report is incorrect, it must be corrected by the credit agency.

4. The debtor may sue for incorrect reports.

10.7 PERFORMANCE OF THE SALES CONTRACT

The Basic Duty of the Seller is to transfer and deliver the goods.

The Basic Duty of the Buyer is to accept and pay for the goods in accordance with the contract.

EXAMPLE

An example of TENDER OF DELIVERY BY THE SELLER follows: The Seller phones the Buyer and tells the Buyer that the computer is at the Seller's store ready to be picked up.

The Place of Tender is important. If it not expressed in the Sales Contract, it is at the seller's place of business. If he has none, then at the seller's home.

Free on Board, Shipping Point means that the goods change hands at the place of shipment.

Free on Board, Destination means that the goods change hands upon arrival at the location of the buyer.

Perfect Tender Rule is that the seller's tender (offer) of performance must conform exactly to the contract.

Modifications of the Perfect Tender Rule follow:

1. **Agreement by the Parties** means that the seller and buyer may agree that the seller can repair or replace defective parts or goods.

2. **Cure by the Seller** can keep the contract in force.

EXAMPLE

The Buyer (Plaintiff) refuses to accept the goods because of some flaw. If the Seller (Defendant) acts immediately and produces the correct goods, the Seller has corrected the flaw.

3. The following is an example of *Installment Contracts*:

The seller delivers the goods in separate lots, and the buyer pays in installments as the goods are received.

Inspection rules are as follows: The buyer may inspect the goods before accepting them. This inspection should be done within reasonable time.

1. Expenses of inspection are usually borne by the buyer.

2. Expenses of inspection may be recovered from the seller if the goods do not conform to the contract of sales.

3. **Exception** is C.O.D. sales. Then the buyer must pay before inspecting the goods.

Rejection rules are as follows: Buyer must notify seller within a reasonable time.

1. **A Non-Merchant Rejector of Goods** has no further obligation with regard to the goods.

2. A **Merchant Rejector of Goods** that are not reclaimed by the seller

   — May store goods to the seller's account.

   — May reship them to the seller.

   — May resell them for the seller's account.

Payment rules are as follows: The Buyer pays at the place designated in the sales contract. (If no place is designated, payment should be made at the time and place where the buyer is to receive the goods.)

Excuses for Nonperformance are:

1. Casualty to Identified Goods. Destruction of these specific goods.

2. Non-Happening of Presupposed Condition caused by strikes, lockouts, shutdown of sources of supply, fire, etc.

3. The following is an example of *Substituted Performance*: If the agreed manner of delivery becomes impractical (railroad goes bankrupt) a substituted manner of delivery (by truck), if commercially reasonable, must be tendered (offered) and accepted.

10.8 REMEDIES

Remedies are the legal means of enforcing a right or redressing a wrong.

Types of Buyer Default are: The Buyer wrongfully rejects the goods. The Buyer fails to make payment. The Buyer repudiates the contract.

Remedies of the Seller are what a seller can do to protect self after buyer default. The Seller can:

1. Withhold delivery of the goods.

2. Stop delivery of the goods by a carrier or other bailee.

3. Identify conforming goods to the contract — separate the goods to be used in the contract from other goods still in the seller's control and resell these to others.

4. Recover damages for nonacceptance or repudiation.

5. Recover the price from the buyer.

6. Recover incidental damages. That is, recover the difference between the resale price and the contract price, transportation, care, and commissions.

7. Cancel the contract.

8. Reclaim goods upon the buyer's insolvency.

Types of Seller Default are: Repudiation, failure to deliver the goods, delivering goods that do not conform to the contract.

Remedies of the Buyer are what a buyer can do when seller defaults. Buyer can: cancel the contract, recover the payment already made, recover damages for nondelivery or repudiation, recover identified goods on the seller's insolvency, sue for replevin to recover specific goods unlawfully held by the seller, sue for specific performance — for a unique item such as a work of art, a racehorse, an heirloom, where money damages are not enough.

A buyer may enforce a "Security Interest" in the goods.

EXAMPLE

The Buyer was required to pay in advance. The goods when finally delivered were not the correct goods mentioned in the contract. The Seller refused to take the goods back. The Buyer may resell the goods but must account to the Seller for any excess of the net proceeds of the resale over the cost and expenses.

A buyer may recover *Incidental Damages*. These are: expenses of inspection, receipt, transportation, care and custody of goods rightfully rejected, and commissions.

10.9 PRODUCT LIABILITY

Product Liability is now the concern of manufacturers as well as wholesalers and retailers. The cost of product liability insurance has skyrocketed because of the explosion of product liability lawsuits and the size of damages awarded in these suits.

Negligence is when a manufacturer is liable to persons injured by the product.

EXAMPLE

Auto firms (Defendants) are sued for manufacturing cars with brakes that lock.

Violation of Statutory Duty is when a manufacturer is not careful about strict branding, labeling, and description of contents laws regarding adulterated, contaminated, or unwholesome products.

Warranties are promises by the seller concerning some aspect of the sale, such as the quality of the goods, the quantity, or the title.

10.10 SECURED TRANSACTIONS

Secured Transactions under the *Uniform Commercial Code* are where a party to the contract gives another valuable goods to hold until the contract is carried out. These valuables are called *Collateral*.

EXAMPLE

A businessman wants a loan from the bank and puts up his inventory as security for the loan.

Security Agreement between debtor and creditor must be in writing, signed by the debtor, and must contain a description of the collateral sufficient to reasonably identify it.

EXCEPTION

If the secured party is in possession of the collateral (banker holds stock certificates that are collateral for the loan) then the agreement need not be written.

A **Security Interest** is created when three events happen:

1. The Debtor signs the *Security Agreement*.

2. The **Secured Party** is given something of value (collateral).

3. The **Debtor** must have rights in the collateral. (Let us say that the Debtor owns stock certificates in Debtor's name which the Debtor hands over to the banker to hold during

the time of the loan. This gives the banker assurance that the debt will be paid.)

Perfection of Security Interest is making the collateral safe from being taken over by third parties, such as creditors in case of the debtor's bankruptcy.

1. The **Secured Party (Banker)** should file a financing statement at the courthouse or other proper government office.

2. Perfection by possession means possessing the collateral. If the Secured Party (Banker) has possession (of the stock certificates) the banker need not file a financing statement.

State Requirements often conflict regarding whether or not it is necessary to file financing statements.

1. States requiring Certificates of Title for autos, mobile homes, trailers, boats (a majority of the states) do not require filing when these assets are put up for collateral. The banker can hold the *Certificate of Title*.

2. States not having Certificates of Titles for autos, mobile homes, trailers, and boats require that agreements be filed in order to protect the secured party.

Default of Debtor can occur in several ways as follows: non-insurance of collateral, removal of collateral, loss or destruction of collateral, bankruptcy.

10.11 CONSUMER LAW

Consumer Law is to protect the consumer against underhanded operators. The **Federal Trade Commission** is empowered to stop false and misleading advertising.

Modern law condemns *Bait And Switch Advertising*. This is the practice of advertising a product at a very low price, then trying to talk the customer into a higher priced product.

It is considered "Bait And Switch" Advertising If:

1. There is Refusal to show the advertised item.

2. There is Disparagement of the advertised item.

3. There is Failure to have the advertised item available in reasonable quantities.

4. There is Refusal to promise delivery of the advertised item within a reasonable time.

5. The company discourages sales personnel from selling advertised products.

Once a complaint is issued, the seller is given a chance to agree to a formal *Cease And Desist Order* from the Federal Trade Commission, or else the seller may be given a chance to informally discontinue the practice, or else the FTC can order *Corrective Advertising*.

Modern Law allows a *Three-Day Cooling Off Period* for door-to-door sales of $25 or more. This is allowed by Federal Trade Commission. If a customer buys a product that the customer does not really want from a high-pressure salesman, the customer has three days to change his or her mind legally.

Modern Law closely monitors Referral Sales and Leases. For example, the buyer will buy at one higher price (say, a set of encyclopedias) with the promise that if the buyer furnishes names and addresses of several friends and any of these friends buy the product, the buyer will get a bonus reduction on the buyer's encyclopedias for each of the friends who buys the product.

The result is that under recent law the giving of names is legal; it is just the price reduction that is now illegal.

Regulation Z of The Federal Reserve System states that lenders must inform borrowers of the finance charge and the annual percentage rate so that they can compare this loan with others.

1. The Finance Charge includes: interest, carrying charge, loan fee, points, finder's fee, appraisal fee, investigation and credit report fee, premiums for required insurance.

2. The finance charges does not include: fees paid public officials, taxes, license fees, certificates of title, registration fees imposed by law, late payment fees, overdraft charges.

3. Credit Cards are now closely regulated. The credit card owner of a *Lost credit card* is now liable for only $50 if this owner:

   — Has an accepted credit card that wa: requested and signed for.

   — Is sure that the card-issuing firm has given the card owner adequate notice of the owner's potential liability.

   — Is sure that the card-issuing company has provided the cardholder with the address of the card-issuing firm.

   — Is dealing with a card issuer who has either the cardholder's signature, photograph, or fingerprints.

— Has agreed that the cardholder can give notice of theft to the card issuer by letter, telegram, radiogram, cablegram, etc.

4. **Balloon Payments** are payments of more than twice the amount of the other installment payments.

   If the agreement has a Balloon Payment, the Consumer has the right to refinance, without penalty, the amount of that payment at the time it is due and the terms of refinancing shall be no less favorable to the consumer than the terms of the original transaction. (Note: This section of the Code has been adopted by only nine states.)

Fair Credit Reporting Act of 1970 regulates Credit Bureaus as follows:

1. When credit bureaus issue reports on a consumer to a business requesting it, this information must be reported also to the particular consumer.

2. The credit bureau (with certain exceptions) must reveal to the consumer all information, except medical information, in its files about the particular consumer.

3. The consumer has an opportunity to make limited corrections regarding the information in the consumer's file at the credit bureau.

4. Federal Trade Commission can take cases to court for persons obtaining information from credit bureaus under false pretenses.

Fair Credit Billing Act (1975) protects customers from *Typical Billing Errors* such as: Customer did not get an extension of credit, some services were undelivered or unaccepted, some payments and/or credits on the bill were incorrect, there were clerical or computation mistakes on the bill.

1. The customer should file a written *Claim of Error* as follows: The *Claim* must be written and received at the creditor's disclosed address. It should give the customer's name and account number (if any) and should indicate that the customer believes there has been a billing error. The Claim should set forth the amount of the error, and should set forth the reasons for the customer's belief.

2. Each creditor must respond to the *Claim of Error* within 30 days.

3. A creditor cannot restrict the customer from using the customer's open-end account during this period of 30 days.

Equal Credit Opportunity Act states that a creditor shall not discriminate against any applicant on the basis of sex or marital status, race, color, religion, national origin, age, or receipt of income from a public assistance program.

Fair Debt Collection Practices Act is a federal act to eliminate abusive debt collection practices.

Purpose of the Fair Debt Collection Practices Act is to regulate third-party debt collectors (usually collection agencies) of overdue accounts.

1. Exceptions to the Act: The original creditor himself or an employee of the original creditor and attorneys.

2. Those subject to the Act: Third party collectors of debts for personal, family, or household purposes.

3. Prohibitions in the Law:

— Collector may not communicate with debtor at an unusual place or time (Midnight phone calls.)

— Collector may not use violence or threat of violence.

— Collector may not use obscene language.

— Collector may not publish a list of persons trying to avoid paying their bills.

— Collector may not resort to excessive or anonymous phone calls.

— Collector may not use collect phone calls or telegrams to conceal the true purpose of the communication.

Federal Trade Commission Improvement Act of 1975 sets up federal minimum standards for warranties, establishes rules for terms and conditions of service contract disclosure.

Interstate Land Sales Full Disclosure Act regulates Realtors. Anyone selling or leasing 50 or more lots of unimproved land as part of a common promotional plan in interstate commerce or by use of the mails must first file a statement of record with the Department of Housing and Urban Development containing detailed information about the land and the developer. The developer must also furnish each purchaser a property report.

Real Estate Settlements Procedure Act of 1975 covers all federally related mortgage loans. Requires disclosure of charges, prohibits kickbacks and splitting of fees except for services actually rendered, limits the amount that a borrower must pay into a special escrow fund for taxes and insurance.

Motor Vehicle Information and Cost Savings Act of 1972 states that all the various elements of the cost of an auto must be disclosed to the buyer. If the odometer has been reset below the true mileage, this fact must be disclosed to the buyer.

Flammable Fabrics Act covers wearing apparel, household furnishings, carpet and rug standards, bedding and mattress standards, and children's no-burn sleepwear standards.

Mail Fraud Statute provides civil and criminal penalties when a party is found to be conducting a scheme or device of obtaining money or property through the mails by means of fraudulent practices.

National Traffic and Motor Vehicle Safety Act of 1966 sets motor vehicle safety standards, tire labeling standards, and notification to auto purchasers and tire and auto parts purchasers of defects discovered by the manufacturer.

REVIEW QUESTIONS

1. How does a Sale differ from a Contract to Sell?
A sale calls for title of goods to pass immediately from the buyer to the seller. A Contract to Sell specifies that title passes at some future time.

2. What is the Uniform Commercial Code?
A series of state laws passed by 49 states governing business and commercial transactions.

3. What is intangible property?
Property which cannot strictly be touched — like patents and copyrights.

4. What is tangible property?

Property which can be touched — like autos, stoves, bicycles.

5. What is barter?

Exchanging goods for goods, without money.

6. Can future goods (like future offspring of a cow) be sold in a valid contract?

No.

7. Are auction sales over $500 legal?

Yes.

8. How does sale on approval differ from sale or return?

Title and risk of loss do not pass to buyer on SALE ON APPROVAL until the passage of a reasonable time. Title and risk of loss do pass immediately to the buyer if there is SALE OR RETURN.

9. What is a C.O.D. sale?

Cash on Delivery. Recipient cannot open the package until he pays the deliverer. This has no effect on when title or risk passes. That is determined by the sales contract.

10. What is a sale by an entrustee?

Selling of goods by a person with whom we have entrusted our goods. Let us say we leave our clothes at the laundry and the laundry sells them. The new owner owns the clothes but we can sue the laundry.

11. Who owns goods left on consignment?

The consignor — the person who left the goods at the store to be sold.

12. What if the consignee goes bankrupt and the consigned goods are taken by the consignee's creditors?

This is legal.

13. If a person purchases a bill of lading or a warehouse receipt in good faith from a person who does not really own the goods, can this purchaser keep the goods?

Yes.

14. How does a warranty differ from a seller's opinion?

A warranty is part of the sales contract while a statement of seller's opinion is not.

15. What is an implied warranty?

A warranty that is guaranteed by law and not necessarily by contract. Example: When food and drink are sold, there is an implied warranty by the seller that the goods are fit for human consumption.

16. If a casual seller sells second-hand or used goods, is there a warranty?

No.

17. If you are hurt by a manufactured product (like a car or a toy) can you sue the manufacturer of one of the component parts?

Yes.

18. Can small loan firms legally charge higher interest rates than banks charge?

Yes.

19. What is usury?

The crime of charging interest rates higher than the state law allows.

20. What branch of the government should be called in to prevent false and deceptive advertising?

The Federal Trade Commission.

21. What truths are important according to the Truth in Lending Act?

The exact yearly interest rate and the total finance charges in dollars.

22. What group is controlled by the Fair Credit Reporting Act?

Credit Bureaus.

23. If the terms of the sales contract are: Free on Board Shipping Point, when does title to the goods pass?

When the goods leave the seller's loading dock.

24. If the terms of the sales contract are: Free on Board Destination, when does title to the goods pass?

When the goods arrive at the buyer's loading dock.

25. What if the buyer rejects the goods and notifies the seller who does not come to pick them up in a reasonable time?

Buyer may sell the goods but must account for them and return any net profit to the seller.

26. If the seller does not carry out his end of the contract, can the buyer sue for specific performance?

Only in cases where money alone will not suffice, as when the item to be purchased is unique: like a racehorse.

27. What is collateral?

Security for a loan.

28. Do financing statements need to be filed by the secured party if the collateral is a car and the state has certificates of title?

No.

29. What is bait and switch advertising?

Low prices advertised on a specific item. When customers arrive at the store, the clerk tries to talk them into a different item.

30. What is a referral sale?

Allowing a customer to purchase an encyclopedia at a cheaper price if some potential customers whom this customer referred to the salesman also buy the product.

31. What is a balloon payment?

A payment of more than twice the amount of the other installment payments.

32. For what purpose is the Fair Credit Billing Act?

Set up to protect customers from improper billing by businesspeople.

33. What is the purpose of the Fair Debt Collection Practices Act?

To protect the rights of debtors from unfair collection practices of third parties — usually collection agencies.

34. What is the purpose of the Interstate Land Sales Full Disclosure Act?

To protect the public from unscrupulous sales practices of some real estate agencies.

35. What is the purpose of the Flammable Fabrics Act?

To protect consumers from buying clothing, household furnishings, carpets, bedding, and sleepwear that might catch fire.

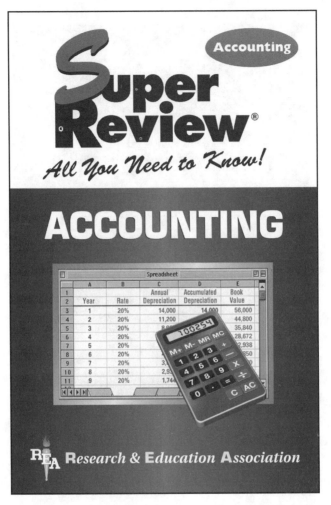

Available at your local bookstore or order directly from us by sending in coupon below.

REA's **Problem Solvers**

The "PROBLEM SOLVERS" are comprehensive supplemental text-books designed to save time in finding solutions to problems. Each "PROBLEM SOLVER" is the first of its kind ever produced in its field. It is the product of a massive effort to illustrate almost any imaginable problem in exceptional depth, detail, and clarity. Each problem is worked out in detail with a step-by-step solution, and the problems are arranged in order of complexity from elementary to advanced. Each book is fully indexed for locating problems rapidly.

ACCOUNTING
ADVANCED CALCULUS
ALGEBRA & TRIGONOMETRY
AUTOMATIC CONTROL
   SYSTEMS/ROBOTICS
BIOLOGY
BUSINESS, ACCOUNTING, & FINANCE
CALCULUS
CHEMISTRY
COMPLEX VARIABLES
DIFFERENTIAL EQUATIONS
ECONOMICS
ELECTRICAL MACHINES
ELECTRIC CIRCUITS
ELECTROMAGNETICS
ELECTRONIC COMMUNICATIONS
ELECTRONICS
FINITE & DISCRETE MATH
FLUID MECHANICS/DYNAMICS
GENETICS
GEOMETRY
HEAT TRANSFER

LINEAR ALGEBRA
MACHINE DESIGN
MATHEMATICS for ENGINEERS
MECHANICS
NUMERICAL ANALYSIS
OPERATIONS RESEARCH
OPTICS
ORGANIC CHEMISTRY
PHYSICAL CHEMISTRY
PHYSICS
PRE-CALCULUS
PROBABILITY
PSYCHOLOGY
STATISTICS
STRENGTH OF MATERIALS &
   MECHANICS OF SOLIDS
TECHNICAL DESIGN GRAPHICS
THERMODYNAMICS
TOPOLOGY
TRANSPORT PHENOMENA
VECTOR ANALYSIS

If you would like more information about any of these books,
complete the coupon below and return it to us or visit your local bookstore.

RESEARCH & EDUCATION ASSOCIATION
61 Ethel Road W. • Piscataway, New Jersey 08854
Phone: (732) 819-8880   **website: www.rea.com**

Please send me more information about your Problem Solver books

Name _____

Address _____

City _____ State _____ Zip _____